HOW TO KEEP YOUR SOUL

HOW TO KEEP YOUR SOUL

A Teen's Guide Against Spells, Curses, Demonic Influences, and Pop culture

Scripture quotations, unless otherwise indicated, are mostly taken from the King James Version and New King James Version of the Bible.

How To Save Your Soul: *A Teen's Guide Against Spells, Curses, Demonic Influences and Pop Culture*

ISBN: 9798395273154

Library of Congress Control Number: 2020919928

Printed in the United States of America.

10 9 8 7 6 5 4 3 2 1

DEDICATION

This book was inspired and written by the Holy Spirit to the youth. Listen to what the Spirit is saying to the churches: Repent, for the Kingdom of God is at hand. "Awake, O' sleeper, and arise from the dead and Christ will shine on you." –Ephesians 5:14

Prayer for the Youth

Lord, I pray that you open their eyes of understanding so that they may know the truth and the truth shall set them free.

> *He preserveth the souls of his saints; he delivereth them out of the hand of the wicked." --Psalm 97:10*

TABLE OF CONTENTS

INTRODUCTION

This world is a fallen creation. We know this by looking all around us. Our contemporary culture delivers false hopes and promises, and we are continually being bombarded with images of this worldly system designed to trap us in physical and material pursuits. The whole world refers to the agents and agencies that govern this world in the spiritual and physical dimensions. We may be familiar with the illuminati or the Freemasons, the Rothschilds, The Club of Rome and other groups who work behind the scenes to control the economic, geopolitical, educational, religious systems, and the entertainment industry, but the real rulers of this world are spiritual forces of evil in the heavenly realms:

> *"For our struggle is not against flesh and blood,*
> *but against the rulers, against the authorities,*
> *against the powers of this dark world and against*
> *the spiritual forces of evil in the heavenly*
> *realms." –Ephesians 6:12*

Therefore, if these evil entities control the world, then how does this affect us? Today, we are subjected to all kinds of filth and immorality that pollute our souls and crush our spirits. We are also victims of the power of evil through wars, persecution, abortions, murders, abuse, hatred etc.... We cannot even escape the influence of evil in our personal lives through unhealthy relationships, pride of life, habits, and addictions. We are a fallen creation in need of redemption and restoration. Therefore, how do we resist temptations, lures, and traps of this world? Jesus admonishes his disciples:

> *"Do not love the world nor the things in the world. If anyone loves the world, the love of the Father is not in him." -- John 2:15*

The apostle Paul writes:

> *"And do not be conformed to this world, but be transformed by the renewing of your mind, so that you may prove what the will of God is, that which is good and acceptable and perfect." –* *Romans 12:2*

I am not saying that we should live in a cave to escape the world, for we are part of the world, but we should not try to imitate or conform (adapt, accept or fit in) with the world and its desires, for the Bible says that *"the world is passing away along with its desires, but whoever does the will of God lives forever"* (1 John 2:17).

It is evident that there is a spiritual dimension, an unseen world that activates the physical world and vice versa. We can activate the spiritual world, too, by our thoughts, actions, and words. There are unseen forces of light and darkness at work all around us, and many are especially fascinated by the spiritual realm because they intuitively understand its power and importance. Many are drawn to the occult in pursuit of the supernatural and the invisible because they are "seekers" by nature. Seekers of truth are souls hungry and thirsty for the truth *"Everyone who thirsts, come to the waters; And you who have no money come, buy and eat. Come, buy wine and milk Without money and without cost"* (Isaiah 55:1). The "waters" are not a reference to drinking water, but the Word of God and the infilling of the Holy Spirit. For example, Paul instructs the church *"Husbands, love your wives, even as Christ also loved the church, and gave himself for it; That he might sanctify and cleanse it with the washing of water by the word"* (KJV Ephesians 5:25-26). The Word sanctifies, cleanses, and renews our minds. It has the power *"to save your souls"* (James 1:21).

The Holy Spirit is also described as water. For example, *"For I will pour out water on the thirsty land and streams on the dry ground; I will pour out My Spirit on your offspring And My blessing on your descendants."* (Isaiah 44:3) In John 4:4-26, Jesus offers the Samaritan woman *living water* that *"whosoever* drinks of that water will *never thirst* and in him will be a *well of water* springing *up into everlasting life.*" This is not H2O; this is a spiritual water that feeds our spirit and soul. This is the source of abundant life. Without this water, we are spiritually dead. Religion or church traditions cannot satisfy the hungry soul.

For example, Samaritans believe that their worship is based on the true religion of the ancient Israelites from before the Babylonian captivity; devout Jews follow the laws of Moses in the Torah; however, both the Samaritans and Jews follow dead religions. In fact, the Protestant church is also a dead religion. Jesus wants born-again, power-filled disciples, or soldiers that will live out their faith. In other words, simply following rules or doctrines or serving in a church does not satisfy our thirst or hunger.

If you feel that you do not fit in the church or culture or have been rejected by the world's standard and are seeking the truth to find your purpose, God has chosen you, for *"God hath chosen the foolish things of the world to confound the wise; and God hath chosen the weak things of the world to confound the things which are mighty"* (1 Corinthians 1:27). Jesus said, *"No one can come to me unless the Father who sent me draws them, and I will raise them up at the last day"* (John 6:44). There are great examples of seekers in the Bible such as King Asa who entered Israel into a covenant to seek after the God of their fathers, with all their heart and soul (2 Chronicles 15:12). As a result, he removed the altars and high places of Israel, even removed his grandmother because she made an Asherah pole. The prophet Azariah spoke to King Asa and said, *"If you seek him, he will be found by you, but if you forsake him, he will forsake you"* (2 Chron. 15:2). Then there's King Josiah. We read that *"In the eighth year of his reign, while he was still young, he began to seek the God of his father*

David. In the twelfth year he began to purge Judah and Jerusalem of high places, Asherah poles, carved idols and cast images" (2 Chronicles 34:3 NIV). He was able to take down Asherah poles and destroy the altars to Baal. We also read that he removed the male prostitutes from the Temple of God, and along with them the sacred horses that were dedicated to the sun (2 Kings 23: 6-7, 11).

In short, this book is for seekers of the truth who hunger for the kingdom of God. Jesus said, *"And ye shall know the truth, and the truth shall make you free"* (John 8:32). When you realize that the powers of this dark world have laid traps for your soul, to deceive and destroy you, and understand that *Jesus has destroyed the works of the devil* (1 John 3:8) and *has overcome the world* (John 16:33), you will have victory over the enemy and *"no weapon forged against you will prevail"* (Isaiah 54:17). But you will have to destroy the "high places," Asherah poles and altars to Baal. In other words, you will have to purge ALL the idols in your life that do not glorify God. This will mean repenting (turning from sin or changing your mind) and asking Jesus to blot out all your iniquity (sinful nature). In other words, if you want to keep your soul, you must lose your sinful life. You must turn away (reject) the seductive entrapments of this life, to preserve your soul. *"Whoever tries to keep their life will lose it, and whoever loses their life will preserve it"* (Luke 17:33).

If you are trapped in the occult, witchcraft, addictions, or other forms of enslavement, I have good news for you: Jesus came not only to *"bring good news to the afflicted"* but *"to bind up the brokenhearted, to proclaim* liberty *to captives and freedom to prisoners"* (Isaiah 61:1). You may have sold your soul to the devil, or allowed the devil legal entrance into your life, but the Lord has already purchased your freedom at the cross, you just need to *"submit yourselves, then, to God. Resist the devil, and he will flee from you* (James 4:7). Resist means to withstand, strive against, or oppose but it is impossible to resist the enemy with our own strength, we must *put on the full armor of God* and take *the sword of the spirit which is the Word of God* (Ephesians 6:13-18). If you are a Christian who has fallen or backslidden, know that God has not forsaken you *"What do you think? If a man owns a hundred sheep, and one of them wanders away, will he not leave the ninety-nine on the hills and go to look for the one that wandered off?"* (Matthew 18:12). God cares for your soul *"not willing that any should perish, but that all should come to repentance."* (2 Peter 3:9).

CHAPTER ONE

The Soul's Substance and The Invisible Realm

"For in him all things were created: things in heaven and on earth, visible and invisible, whether thrones or powers or rulers or authorities; all things have been created through him and for him." –Colossians 1:16 NIV

There is an invisible realm from which all great ideas, revolutionary inventions, good and evil originate. Man's mind is finite and limited since the fall. Science has concluded that average humans only use 2 percent of their brain capacity, while geniuses like Einstein may have used up to 10 percent. Before the fall, Adam and Eve had 100 percent brain capacity and lived in two realms or dimensions: physical and spiritual. The tree of the knowledge of good and evil and the tree of life produced spiritual fruit that had spiritual consequences. Likewise, the games that you play, the programs that you watch or games that you *consume (spend time, energy)*, produce spiritual fruit (thoughts, emotions, and actions). The programs or videos you *consume* also produce a kind of fruit in life whether good or evil. In Luke 11:34, Jesus said,

"Your eyes are a lamp that provides light for your body. When your eye is good, your whole body is filled with light. But when it is bad, your body is filled with darkness. Make sure that the light you think you have is not actually darkness. If you are filled with light, with no dark corners, then your whole life will be radiant, as though a floodlight were filling you with light."

If you are watching, listening, and consuming ungodly music, programs, movies, games, or videos, you must repent. Your eyes and ears are the gates to your soul. If you *consume* filth, you fill your soul with darkness. As a living soul, you can produce good fruit or unclean fruit. You can *consume* unwholesome music and produce unwholesome thoughts, ideas, and words. Whatever you *consume*, you will produce. For example, if you are addicted to pornography or fantasy, you will produce unclean thoughts, words and even actions. Masturbation is a sin produced by unclean thoughts. In Matthew 5:28, Jesus says, *"But I say unto you, that whosoever looketh on a woman to lust after her hath committed adultery with her already in his heart."* In other words, if you lust or fantasize after any woman or man (real or

[20]

imaginary), it is the sin of adultery. You must repent (stop) and ask the LORD to cleanse your eye gate and soul (heart). To live, you must die to yourself (selfish desires, ambitions, or pursuits) daily.

The enemy of our soul has so blinded this generation with distractions and fantasy that we have lost the true meaning and purpose of life. Our soul was not created to play video games eight hours a day but to glorify and honor God. You were not created to idle away; your soul was created to walk and commune with God like Adam did in the garden. What is the soul? Every living creature has a soul. In this chapter, we will learn the purpose and origin of the soul and its connection to our spirit and body, and we will learn why the soul is so valuable to God and so sought after by the devil.

The Invisible Realm

In Genesis 2:7, we see that *"the Lord God formed man of the dust of the ground and breathed into his nostrils the breath of life; and man became a living soul."* God formed the male and female spirits after his likeness and then formed man's physical body from the dust of the ground and took out the female counterpart from his rib. In other words, the spiritual world was created before the physical world. This is reiterated throughout the Bible. For example:

> *"For by him were all things created that are in heaven, and that are in earth, visible and invisible, whether they be thrones, or dominions, or principalities, or powers: all things were created by him, and for him."* –Colossians 1:16

> *"For the invisible things of him from the creation of the world are clearly seen, being understood by the things that are made, even his eternal power and Godhead; so that they are without excuse. –* Romans 1:20

Furthermore, Genesis 2:5 KJV, proves the invisible world existed before the physical when it states: *"And every plant of the field before it was in the earth, and every herb of the field, before it grew: for the Lord God had not caused it to rain upon the earth, and there was not a man to till the ground."* So, God created man in the spirit before he formed him from the dust and breathed life in him, but he also created the plants and herbs of the field before they appeared on the earth.

Now, in the New Testament, Luke 10:19, Jesus bestows on "redeemed man" a new power: *"authority over serpents and scorpions, and upon all the power of the enemy.*" "Serpents and scorpions" are types of spiritual powers. In Genesis 3, we see the "*serpent*" deceived Eve and in Revelations 9:3 "*power was given them as the scorpions of the earth have power.*" Therefore, serpents and scorpions refer to evil forces or demonic entities, not creatures.

If we are going to keep our souls or protect ourselves from the attacks of the enemy: sorcery, witchcraft, spells or other forms of curses and traps, we must arm ourselves with the truth. You see, Jesus has given redeemed man "*all the power of the enemy.*" This means that Jesus has not only restored mankind's relationship with God, but his position, dominion, and authority over the visible and invisible realms of creation. We were restored in God's image or likeness having authority, dominion, and power over the seen and unseen realms.

Substance of the Soul

According to Genesis 1:7, "*God formed man of the dust of the ground and breathed into his nostrils the breath of life:*" In Hebrew, "breath of life" means a *living creation or the breath of God imparting life and wisdom.* Wow, do you understand what this means? We are living beings created by the almighty God. We have been "imparted" life and divine attributes; Therefore,

[23]

the substance of our body is the dust of the ground, and the substance of our soul is God's breath of life or divine substance. The Bible distinguishes between the spirit, soul, and body:

> *"Then the dust will return to the earth as it was, and the spirit will return to God who gave it." –Ecclesiastes 3:21*

> *"For just as the body without the spirit is dead, so also faith without works is dead." –James 2:26*

> *"Therefore, we do not lose heart, but though our outer man is decaying, yet our inner man is being renewed day by day." –2 Corinthians 4:16*

Anatomy of the Spirit

In Ecclesiastes 12:6, Solomon writes *"Remember him— before the silver cord is severed, and the golden bowl is broken; before the pitcher is shattered at the spring, and the wheel broken at the well."* The *silver cord,* much like the umbilical cord, connects the soul and spirit to the body. When the cord or connection is severed, we die. The *golden bowl or pitcher* is the dwelling place of the Holy Spirit. This *pitcher* is also referred to as the *fountain*: *"But the water that I shall give him will become in him a fountain of water springing up into everlasting life"* (John

4:14). This is where the spirit and soul communicate or connect: *"Create in me a clean heart O God and renew a right spirit within me"* (Psalm 51:10). The *wheels* are the garments that cover the spirit man. These garments can become defiled (dirty or unclean) through unrepentance, *"Thou hast a few names even in Sardis which have not defiled their garments; and they shall walk with me in white: for they are worthy"* (Revelation 3:4). This is not a physical garment or robe, but a spiritual one. Those dressed in *white garments* represent the righteous made clean by the blood of the lamb. Those without garments are the unsaved or backslidden, *"Behold, I come as a thief. Blessed is he that watcheth, and keepeth his garments, lest he walk naked, and they see his shame"* (Revelation 16:15 KJV). Nakedness is associated with the old sinful nature: *"I am overwhelmed with joy in the LORD my God! For he has dressed me with the clothing of salvation and draped me in a robe of righteousness"* (Isaiah 61:10).

The Soul and the Spirit

What is the difference between the soul and the spirit? The simple Biblical answer is found in Genesis. The living soul is what makes man a man. The soul has a mind, will and emotions and it is deeply interconnected with our physical mind, thoughts, and imagination. The spirit connects us with the invisible world or heavenly places. *"And God raised us up with Christ and seated us with him in the heavenly realms in Christ Jesus"* (Ephesians 2:6). In the New Testament, Paul states, *"For who has known the mind of the Lord that he may instruct him? But we have the mind of Christ"* (1 Corinthians 2:15). How can we have the mind of Christ? Christ communicates with our spirit mind and our soul, but the physical mind is not able to comprehend it: *"The disciples did not understand any of this. Its meaning was hidden from them, and they did not know what he was talking about"* (Luke 18:34).

The spirit of an unbeliever is dead and cannot perceive the invisible or spiritual world, but for the believer in Christ, his spirit man is born-again and perceives the spiritual world or Kingdom of Heaven; however, the body and soul must submit to the Holy Spirit: *"But all who are being led by the Spirit of God, these are sons of God"* (Romans 8:14). The Holy Spirit speaks through the spirit man, and the soul interprets or transmits the message. We can communicate with the Spirit of God through the gift of *unknown tongues*. When we are born-again, God gives us the gift of the Holy Spirit and *unknown tongues* to speak directly to Him bypassing our understanding: *"For he that speaketh in an unknown tongue speaketh not unto men, but unto God for no man understandeth him; howbeit in the spirit he speaketh mysteries"* (1 Corinthians 14:2). In other words, this is a private one-on-one conversation with God, and no one, not even our own flesh or any demon can understand what we say.

Thus, when we become *born-again*, the Holy Spirit comes to live inside of us: *"Do you not know that your bodies are temples of the Holy Spirit, who is in you, whom you have received from God? You are not your own; you were bought at a price. Therefore, honor God with your bodies"* (1 Corinthians 6:19-20). The body is sacred to God; therefore, we must not sin against it, so *"that each one of you know how to control his own body in holiness and honor"* (1 Thessalonians 4:4). We must be careful to not grieve or bring sorrow to the Holy Spirit, *"And do not grieve the Holy Spirit of God, with whom you were sealed for the day of redemption"* (Ephesians 4:30). We bring sorrow to the Holy Spirit when we disobey or rebel against Him. Disobedience and rebellion bring soul loss and trauma.

Clearly, the soul suffers loss and emotional pain: *"My soul is greatly troubled; But You, O LORD—how long?"* (Psalm 6:3) and *"My soul loathes my life; I will give free course to my complaint; I will speak in the bitterness of my soul"* (Job 10:1). Both the spirit and the soul can be grieved. For example, Job cried out to God, *"Therefore I will not restrain my mouth; I will speak in the anguish of my spirit; I will complain in the bitterness of my soul"*

(Job 7:11). Thus, the condition of the spirit and soul affect the body, *"For our soul is bowed down to the dust; Our body clings to the ground"* (Psalm 44:25). In addition, the soul hungers and thirst for spiritual food: *"For He satisfies the longing soul and fills the hungry soul with goodness"* (Psalm 107:9).

To restore our souls and renew (repair) our spirit mind, we must meditate on the Word, *"Do not conform to the pattern of this world but be transformed by the renewing of your mind. Then you will be able to test and approve what God's will is—his good, pleasing, and perfect will"* (Romans 12:2 NIV). According to the Bible, the *"the word of God is alive and active. Sharper than any double-edged sword, it penetrates even to dividing soul and spirit, joints, and marrow; it judges the thoughts and attitudes of the heart"* (Hebrews 4:12). Now, the soul and spirit have a heart *"For out of the heart proceed evil thoughts, murders, adulteries, fornications, thefts, false witness, blasphemies"* (Matthew 15:19). How does sin enter the heart of man? For this, we must understand our sinful and deprived nature after the fall.

The Spirit of an Unbeliever is Dead

Now, it is important to understand that the spirit of an unbeliever is dead. This is because of man's fallen state after disobeying God: *"But of the tree of knowledge of good and evil, thou shalt not eat of it: for in the day that thou eatest thereof thou shalt surely die"* (Genesis 2:18) Adam and Eve did not physically die, but spiritually died after disobeying God. Their spiritual connection to God was severed, but Jesus' redemptive work on the cross restored man's position and authority, so now, God speaks to our redeemed soul and "born again" spirit. *"Truly, truly, I say to you, unless one is born of water and the Spirit, he cannot enter the kingdom of God. That which is born of the flesh is flesh, and that which is born of the Spirit is spirit"* (John 3:5-6).

To review, God created man's spirit in His image and likeness first, then he formed (fashioned) man of the dust of the ground and breathed life into him. The spirit was created by the Word of God, the body was fashioned or formed by the hand of God, and the soul (life) was imparted by the breath of God. We were dead spiritually through Adam's sin, but Jesus came to give us life again *"the first man Adam became a living being the last Adam, a life-giving spirit."* Jesus was the last Adam. He was a perfect (sinless) man who shed his blood as a ransom price for many (Mathew 20:28). Adam was created perfect or without sin

[29]

who was to live forever, but "sold" himself and his offspring into slavery to sin and death (Romans 7:14). However, God felt compassion for Adam's descendants in their hopelessness, so God devised a plan to legally save and restore him to his former state. It would require a sin offering or blood sacrifice of an innocent, sinless man. Jesus' sacrifice paid the ransom price. The Bible says, "*Just as through the disobedience of the one man (Adam) many were made sinners, so also through the obedience of the one person (Jesus Christ) many will be made righteous.*" (Romans 5:19). Therefore, we were once dead in our spirits, and prisoners of sin and death, but Jesus came to resurrect our spirits and redeem our souls. Do you understand what this means? Jesus suffered one of the most horrific death sentences in history, death by crucifixion, to pay a ransom in exchange for our souls.

Jesus' Soul an Offering for Sin

There is evidence to show that Jesus not only suffered the bruising of his body but soul. According to Isaiah 53:11-12, the Father made Jesus' soul an offering for sin. In verses 11-12, the Hebrew transliteration for "*soul*" or "*nephesh*" means "breath." The Father saw the "*travail*" of his soul (*breath*) and was satisfied. The word "*travail*" in the Hebrew-Chaldee Lexicon means "*heavy labour.*" Under the Mosaic Law, the sin offering was made by sacrificing an unblemished (spotless) young bull or lamb and pouring its blood at the base of the altar. The fat of the sin offering was then removed and burned on the altar. This is a picture of what happened to Jesus at Calvary:

> *"Yet it pleased the LORD to bruise him: he hath put him to grief: when thou make his soul an offering for sin, he shall see his seed, he shall prolong his days, and the pleasure of the LORD shall prosper in his hand. He shall see the travail of his soul, and shall be satisfied: by his knowledge shall my righteous servant justify many: for he shall bear their iniquities" —Isaiah 53:11-12*

There are many scholars who believe that Jesus' death at Calvary was the *finished work of Jesus ministry* and quote John 19:30 NIV, "*It is finished.*" In the Greek, the word finished means "paid in full," so Jesus was done; yet the Scriptures show that He descended into the Earth, and on the third day, rose again. Jesus was resurrected from the dead. Some argue that he was in Abraham's bosom or paradise on the other side of Sheol; however, both Matthew 12:40 and Luke 11:31 reference Jesus descending into Sheol (hell): "*For as Jonah was three days and three nights in the belly of a huge fish, so the Son of Man will be three days and three nights in the heart of the earth.*" Sheol (hell) is in the center of the Earth where the wicked are sent for punishment. In Psalms 16:10, David prophesizes about Jesus, *"For You will not leave my soul in Sheol, nor will You allow Your Holy One to see corruption."* Here, we see that Jesus' soul was in hell, not paradise with the righteous. The Bible also records that Jesus *"poured out his soul to death and was numbered with the transgressors (sinners)"* Isaiah 53:12). Again, David prophesizes Jesus' descent into Sheol and ascent into heaven, *"If I ascend into heaven, you are there; If I make my bed in hell, behold, you are there"* (Psalm 139:8).

According to Ecclesiastics 12:7, Solomon suggests the spirit of man returns to God and the body returns to the earth, *"Then shall the dust return to the earth as it was: and the spirit shall return unto God who gave it."* So, when Jesus cried out, *"Father, into your hands I commit my spirit,"* (Luke 23:46), he was not only quoting Psalms or fulfilling scripture, but he was also entrusting his spirit man to God. Similarly, when we breathe our last breath, our body will return to the ground, our spirit will return to God who gave it, but our soul will either be burned in the fire of judgment or rest into eternal life: *"And these will go away into eternal punishment, but the righteous into eternal life"* (Mathew 25:46).

Be Alert and of Sober Mind

Please understand that a soul can be tortured during its lifetime, but the Lord came *"to destroy the devil's works"* (1 John 3:8) and through his sacrifice on the cross, he gave us authority over *"all the power of the enemy"* (Luke 10:19). The devil is real and wants to take your soul captive. The apostle Peter warns *"Be alert and of sober mind. Your enemy the devil prowls around like a roaring lion looking for someone to devour"* (1 Peter 5:8). This is a spiritual attack on your soul. If you are under the influence of drugs, alcohol, or the occult, you are not *"of sober mind,"* and this means that you have opened yourself up to demonic possession or influence. To illustrate, you are a fortified city under attack. When you take drugs, dabble in witchcraft or intentionally sin, you leave the gates of your city wide open for the enemy to come in and destroy. When you suffer *"heartbreak,"* the devil also storms in the city gates. It is not that your heart (soul) is physically breaking, but that your soul fragments. That is why Solomon, the smartest person in history, writes in Proverbs 4:23, *"Above all else, guard your heart, for everything you do flows from it."* The "heart" is your soul. But I have good news for you, when you accept Jesus as Lord and Savior, He guards and protects your heart and mind, *"And the peace of God, which transcends all understanding, will guard your hearts and your minds in Christ Jesus"* (Philippians 4:7). The peace of God refers the *tranquil state of a soul assured of its*

[33]

salvation through Christ, and so fearing nothing from God; therefore, for you to be set free of curses, addictions, spells, and demonic influences, you MUST of your own *free will* do the following:

1. Declare with your words that Jesus is Lord and Savior.

2. Confess ALL your sins (secret sins, rebellions, thoughts, attitudes, beliefs, judgments) before God and REPENT (turn from ALL sins).

3. Throw out all cursed objects (amulets, jewelry, pentagrams, witchcraft paraphernalia, candles, ceremonial tools, books, video games, apps)

4. Claim the blood of Christ over yourself, home, and family.

5. Ask the Lord for the Holy Spirit to dwell in you.

6. Praise God and thank Him for his forgiveness.

7. Ask God to give you a hunger or thirst for the Word.

8. Set some time to read and meditate on the Word daily.

10. Put away all distractions (Phone, TV, Games)

11. Guard your eyes, ears, and tongue from evil.

12. Listen to praise and worship music.

13. Pray continually.

14. Find pastors or elders of the church to pray over you.

15. Seek the Kingdom of God above all else.

Prayer of Protection Over the Soul

In the precious name of Jesus, I believe you paid a ransom for my soul. Blot out my transgressions and iniquity. Create in me a pure heart, O God, and renew a steadfast spirit within me. Father, I commend my body, soul, and spirit into your hands. Unto thee, O Lord, do I lift my soul. O my God, I trust in thee: let me not be ashamed, let not mine enemies' triumph over me. You restoreth my soul and leadeth me in the paths of righteousness for your name's sake. Gather not my soul with sinners, nor my life with bloody men. O keep my soul and deliver me. O Lord my God, I cried unto thee, and thou has brought up my soul from the grave: thou hast kept me alive that I should not go to the pit. For in the time of trouble, you shall hide me in the secret of your tabernacle and set me up upon a rock. Plead my cause, O Lord, with them that strive with me: fight against them that fight against me. Let them be confounded and put to shame that seek after my soul: let them be turned back and brought to confusion that devise my hurt. The sorrows of death compassed me, and the floods of ungodly men made me afraid but, in my distress, you delivered me from my strong enemy, and from them which hated me; for they were too strong for me. The Lord is my shepherd; I shall not want. He restoreth my soul: he leadeth me in the paths of righteousness for his name's sake. Yea, though I walk through the valley of the shadow of death, I will fear no evil: or thou art with me; thy rod and thy staff they comfort me. Thou preparest a table before me in the presence of mine enemies: thou anointest my head with oil; my cup runneth over.

-- Book of Psalms

CHAPTER TWO

The Spirit, Soul, and Body Connection

"Now may the God of peace Himself sanctify you completely; and may your whole spirit, soul and body be preserved blameless at the coming of our Lord Jesus Christ."

—1 Thessalonians 5:23

Our spirit is connected to our soul and often communicates with our soul through dreams, ideas, thoughts, and impressions. Did you know that many creative ideas or inventions throughout history have come from dreams or the mysterious parts of the brain, connected to imagination or the spirit realm? For example, Einstein's theory of relativity E= mc2 came to him in a dream. Niels Bohr, the father of quantum mechanics, dreamt of the nucleus of the atom with electrons spinning around it. In 1845, Elias Howe discovered the eye of the needle and the first sewing machine in a dream where he was being pursued by warrior savages carrying long spears pierced near the head. Scientists still have not fully understood the link between dreams and the brain.

However, according to the Bible, God uses our dreams to bring instruction, prophecy, or warning. Dreams are produced through our subconscious minds (or the spirit), bypassing our mind, emotions, and social constructs. For example, in 2013, when I was preparing to move to Florida to care for my mother, I had a dream of great ocean waves crashing into the back of my mother's home, and in the next moment of the dream, I was in her home sweeping fish skeletons from the water damage. Unfortunately, I dismissed the dream at the time, but I later realized this was a warning to my soul about the turbulent, negative emotions I would experience and the revelation of ugly family secrets during my two years stay.

Dreams and Visions

In the Bible, God speaks to Joseph in a dream revealing prophetic events: "*I had another dream, and this time the sun and moon and eleven stars were bowing down to me*" (Genesis 27: 9). Here, Joseph predicts that he would become second in command to Pharaoh during a time of famine for the purposes of saving the tribes of Israel. In the book of Daniel, God shows Daniel four beasts (kingdoms) that would rise from the sea (spiritual world): "*I saw in my vision by night, and behold, the four winds of the heaven strove upon the great sea*" (Daniel 7:2). In 2 Corinthians 1-2, The Apostle Paul describes a vision where he was caught up to the third heaven "*whether in the body, I cannot tell: or whether out of the body, I cannot tell: God knoweth.*" Paul had a supernatural experience where his soul was translated to the third heaven. Similarly, in the book of Revelations, the Apostle John was caught up to heaven and received an open vision of the end times. So, it is possible to soul travel while your body remains in an unconscious state.

Seated in Heavenly Places

Similarly, it is possible for one's spirit to be raised up in heavenly realms: "*And God raised us up with Christ and seated us with him in the heavenly realms in Christ Jesus*" (Ephesians 2:6). Jesus' sacrifice on the cross allows us direct access to the throne of God, and just like Adam and Eve had access to both the physical and spiritual planes, we too have access to heavenly realms. If you are dabbling in drugs, witchcraft, or the occult, you may have had out-of-body-experiences or encountered supernatural phenomena. Many new agers and mystics experience astral projection, sleep paralysis or lucid dreaming, but these types of experiences are forbidden by God and represent false imitations of true heavenly experiences, encounters, or visitations.

According to the Bible, there are three heavens: Paul was taken up in the spirit to the third heaven and writes: *"I know a man in Christ who fourteen years ago was caught up to the third heaven—whether in the body or out of the body I do not know, God knows" –2 Corinthians 12:2.* In Genesis 1:20, the first heaven is our sky: *"And God said, 'Let the waters swarm with swarms of living creatures, and let birds fly above the earth across the expanse of the heavens."* The second heaven comprises of principalities of evil in the heavenly realms. (Ephesians 6:12). The third heaven is the Kingdom of Heaven where God's throne room resides.

Therefore, our spirit and soul can travel in the spiritual realms of the 2nd or 3rd heaven. Our spirit and soul have spiritual eyes, ears, nose, heart, and mind; therefore, we can see, hear, smell, feel and think in the spirit realm as well. People who have died and gone to hell have recorded smelling rotting flesh, felt the stifling heat of hot gases, and described people burning in a river of fire or pyroclastic flow. Likewise, many who have died and gone to heaven report hearing choirs of angels singing praises to God, smelling wonderful aromas, and seeing streets of gold. Our spirit and soul can even be in various places at once.

The War Between the Flesh and the Spirit

Similarly, our spirit can be in direct opposition to our flesh (body): *"For the flesh desires what is contrary to the Spirit, and the Spirit contrary to the flesh"* (Galatians 5:17); therefore, as Christians, we are to *die* to the desires and lusts of the flesh and be governed by the spirit: *"The mind governed by the flesh is death, but the mind governed by the Spirit is life and peace"* (Romans 8:6 NIV). How do we deny the desires and lusts of the flesh? We must starve the cravings of the flesh by living in the spirit. For example, when we fast (abstain from food), we are weakening the flesh and strengthening the spirit, *"So I say, walk by the Spirit, and you will not gratify the desires of the flesh"* (Galatians 5:16). We are also to worship in the spirit, *"God is a spirit, and his worshippers must worship in the Spirit and in truth"* (John 4:24). When we are led by the spirit of God dwelling in us, *"The Spirit himself testifies with our spirit that we are God's children"* (Romans 8:16). To subdue the flesh, we should command our body, soul, and spirit man to submit to the will of the Father and become living sacrifices. What does this mean? It means that we must die to our will (self) and let His will be done in our lives. When we submit to the will of the Father in humble obedience, we put to death the works of the flesh (our plans, decisions, desires, and ambitions) and join ourselves to the *mind* of Christ: *"For, "Who can know the LORD's thoughts? Who knows enough to teach him?" But we understand these things, for we have the mind, of Christ"* (1 Corinthians 2:16). In other words, we become one with Christ: *"But the one who joins himself to the Lord is one spirit with Him"* (1 Corinthians 6:17).

The Temple of God

Once you become a believer in Christ Jesus, your spirit man is activated, and the Holy Spirit comes to dwell in you, speaks with your spirit and intercedes on your behalf: *"Do you not know that you are God's temple and that God's spirit dwells in you?"* (1 Corinthians 3: 16).

God called Moses to Mount Sinai and in an open vision, Moses was instructed to replicate or build a tabernacle or Holy temple. The temple consisted of an outer court, inner court and Holy of Holies or inner sanctum. The outer court had a brazen alter made of shittim wood overlaid with horns at each corner and was used by the Israelites for daily sacrifices and the atonement of sin (Exodus 27:1); the bronze laver was used by the priests for cleansing and purification rites (Exodus 30:17-20); the inner court had various instruments: the lampstand, the table of show bread and the altar of incense. The lampstand represents the 7 spirits of God (Exodus 25:31). The table of show bread or unleavened bread was a type and shadow of the Word of God or the true bread of life, Jesus Christ (Exodus 25:23-30; 26:35). The altar of incense was kept burning continually and symbolized prayers offered up to God (Exodus 30:1). Separating the inner court and the Holy of Holies was a veil or curtain (Exodus 26:31-35).

To better understand this, the outer court represents our body; the inner court is our soul, and the Holy of Holies is our spirit communing with God. Therefore, the veil (curtain) was symbolic of our separation from God. In the Holy of Holies, only the High Priest could enter to sprinkle blood upon the Mercy Seat of the Ark of the Covenant to make atonement for Israel's sins and receive instructions from God. The Ark of the Covenant (Exodus 26:33) contained the golden pot that had manna, and Aaron's rod that budded, and the tablets of the covenant.

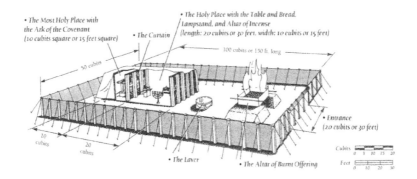

When the temple veil was torn in two from top to bottom after the death of Jesus Christ (Matthew 27:51), it symbolized the end of the old covenant, and the beginning of a new one. The new covenant represents man reconciled to God and no separation between God and man. What does this mean for us today? It means we have access to God. Jesus Christ, our high priest, sprinkled his own blood on the Mercy Seat of the Ark of the Covenant to make atonement for our sins (1 John 2:2). Therefore, we are saved through the blood of Jesus: *"God presented Christ as a sacrifice of atonement, through the shedding of his blood—"* (Romans 3:25).

The Holy Spirit intercedes on our behalf bypassing our limited understanding. The Latin origin of intercede "cedere" means "to go between," so the Holy Spirit goes between our soul and spirit to help us pray.

> *"Likewise, the Spirit helps us in our weakness. For we do not know what to pray for as we ought, but the Spirit himself intercedes for us with groanings too deep for words. And he who searches hearts knows what the mind of the Spirit is, because the Spirit intercedes for the saints according to the will of God" –Romans 8:26-27*

We are the tabernacle of God. The Father communes with us through our spirit man because God is spirit. To hear his voice, we must crucify the carnal mind (flesh). If we do not crucify the flesh, we grieve (offend) the spirit:

> *"And grieve not the holy Spirit of God, whereby ye are sealed unto the day of redemption. Let all bitterness, and wrath, and anger, and clamour, and evil speaking, be put away from you, with all malice." –Ephesians 4:30-31*

We grieve the Holy Spirit when we are disobedient, stubborn, rebellious, wrathful, bitter, jealous, argumentative, unkind, disrespectful, and selfish. We must repent of our words, thoughts, and actions immediately, or we will open the door to the enemy, and he will have legal access to our lives.

The Holy Spirit convicts us of sin, so that we may repent and have a right standing with Abba, our Father; however, when we do not listen to the promptings of the Spirit or resist Him due to selfishness, pride or unforgiveness, we silence Him. This is the reason some Christians cannot hear the voice of God or the Holy Spirit. We must repent (turn around) to have right standing. If we do not turn from our rebellion, Satan, our accuser, *"For the accuser of our brothers and sisters, who accuses them before our*

God day and night, has been hurled down" (Revelation 12:10), will have a legal right to hold our soul in captivity.

Prayer of Submission:

Lord, I pray that the God of peace, himself sanctify me completely and may my whole spirit, soul and body be kept sound and blameless at the coming of our Lord Jesus Christ (1 Thessalonians 5:25). Wash my robes (spirit, soul, and body) and make them white, so that I may have the right to the tree of life and may enter the city (3rd Heaven) by the gates (Revelation 22:14). Redeem my life from the pit (death) and crown me with lovingkindness and tender mercies (Psalm 103:4). I submit my will to your will Father. Yet not My will, but Yours be done (Luke 22:42). My old self has been crucified with Christ. It is no longer I who live, but Christ lives in me. So, I live in this earthly body by trusting in the Son of God who loved me and gave himself for me (Galatians 2:20). I live by the Spirit and put to death the deeds of the body (Romans 8:13). I present my body as a living and holy sacrifice, acceptable to God, which is my spiritual service of worship. I am not conformed to this world, but transformed by the renewing of my mind, so that I may prove what the will of God is, that which is good and acceptable and perfect (Romans 12: 1-2). I do not lose heart, but though my outer man is decaying, my inner man is being renewed day by day (2 Corinthians 4:16).

CHAPTER THREE

The Fragmentation of the Soul

"He restoreth my soul: he leadeth me in the paths of righteousness for his name's sake." —Psalm 23:3

The soul can be fragmented (broken) and imprisoned. We see evidence of this in the life of King David and Job. David cried out to the LORD, *"Save me from all them that persecute me, and deliver me: Lest he tear my soul like a lion, rending it in pieces, while there is none to deliver"* (Psalm 71-2). Here, David is referring to evil spirits that tear at men's souls to trap and torment. Thus, the soul may be persecuted and tortured: *"For the enemy has persecuted my soul"* (Psalm 143:3); the soul can be captured and imprisoned: *"Bring my soul out of prison, That I may praise Your name"* (Psalm 142:7). In Psalm 57:4, King David pleads with God for the protection of his soul, *"Keep my soul, and deliver me: Let me not be ashamed, for I put my trust in You"* (Psalm 25:20). Remember, the soul's substance is ethereal (celestial), not physical; however, the soul can see, hear, smell, taste, touch; it has a mind, heart (emotions) and will. For example, in Luke 16:19-31, we read the story of a certain rich man and a beggar named Lazarus. It came to pass that the beggar died and was carried by the angels to Abraham's bosom in paradise, but the rich man also died and was buried, *"And in hell he lift up his eyes, being in torments, and seeth Abraham afar off, and Lazarus in his bosom. And he cried and said, Father Abraham, have mercy on me, and send Lazarus, that he may dip the tip of his finger in water, and cool my tongue; for I am tormented in this flame."* The rich man had all his senses and was able to see Lazarus from afar and feel the burning flames.

Pain and Trauma

The enemy hooks and traps souls in sin, trauma, pain, and ungodly covenants: *"Thorns (hooks) and snares (traps) are in the way of the perverse; He who guards his soul will be far from them"* (Proverbs 22:5-6). Grief and deep despair cause the soul to break. For example, King David grieves over his sins and many afflictions, *"I am feeble and severely broken; I groan because of the turmoil of my heart"* (Psalm 38: 8). Also, *unforgiveness, bitterness, anger* poison and enslave the soul: *"For I see that you are poisoned by bitterness and captive to iniquity"* (Acts 8:23).

Hence, a soul can be under the power of sin and bound (chained) in iniquity. Trauma (wounds) can also ensnare the soul. In the case of Job, God allowed his faith to be tested through a series of tragic events including the sudden death of all his children and sickness to his body , so he cried out, *"And now my soul is poured out because of my [plight'] The days of my affliction take hold of me"* (Job 30;16). Thus, the righteous are prime targets of the enemy, *"For without because they have hidden their net in a pit for me. Without cause they have dug a pit for my soul"* (Psalm 35:7).

To heal the brokenness of our soul, we must identify the source of the pain or trauma. If our mind has concealed it or compartmentalized it, we need to ask the LORD to reveal the trauma or pain to us for restoration and healing. I suggest attending a healing service, or asking your local pastor or elders of the church to pray over you; "Is anyone among you sick? *Let them call the elders of the church to pray over them and anoint them with oil in the name of the LORD"* (James 5:14). This is not a sickness of the body, but of the soul. Understand that the LORD wants to heal you, and maybe you might not know how to pray, so the Holy Spirit intercedes on your behalf:

> *The Spirit helps us in our weakness. We do not*
> *know what we ought to pray for, but the Spirit*

himself intercedes for us through wordless groans.
And he who searches our hearts knows the mind of
the Spirit, because the Spirit intercedes for God's
people in accordance with the will of God." Ask the
Holy Spirit to intercede and pray for you, and you
will be healed. –Romans 8:26-27

If you learn the source of the trauma or pain, it is important to confess it and forgive the perpetrators. Forgiveness will heal the trauma and restore your soul. Forgiveness is not a feeling, but an action. Jesus said, *"And whenever you stand praying, forgive, if you have anything against anyone, so that your Father also who is in heaven may forgive you your trespasses"* (Mark 11:25). We are to forgive others as God has forgiven us, *"Bearing with one another and, if one has a complaint against another, forgiving each other; as the LORD has forgiven you, so you also must forgive"* (Colossians 3:13). This is vital in the restoration and healing process.

Pray this prayer:

LORD Jesus, I release - (name the perpetrators) for the pain and trauma caused in my life. Today, I choose to forgive - (name the perpetrators) for hurting me because I realize that I, too, am a sinner who has violated God's commandments and need His forgiveness. I confess - (name your sins) and repent. Blot my transgressions from the record and write my name in the Lamb's Book of Life. I curse the root of all bitterness, rage, anger, malice, brawling, slander, or word curses in my heart. Heal and restore my heart (soul). Take your fiery sword and sever any ungodly soul ties or covenants. Release me from any demonic oppression or captivity. I ask for the gift of the Holy Spirit to help me pray and intercede on my behalf. I receive the fruits of the spirit: love, joy, peace, forbearance, kindness, goodness, and faithfulness.

The Power of Words

Words have the power to bless, but they also have the power to curse. In the age of social media, we see the power of words used to shame and mock. In today's culture, cyberbullying has become commonplace. In fact, according to the Pew Research Center, 59 percent of U.S. teens have been bullied or harassed online. In many of these cases, it has led to the victims committing suicide. Remember, *we struggle not against flesh and blood, (other people) but against principalities, against powers, against rulers of the darkness of this world, against spiritual wickedness in high places*" (Ephesians 6:12) that want to destroy us through *offense* or *word curses;* therefore, "*let us not be ignorant of Satan's devices* (weapons) *lest Satan should take advantage of us*" (2 Corinthians 2:11). So how do we respond to word curses or offense? Jesus said, *"Bless those who persecute you; bless and do not curse"* (Romans 12:14).

The Bible warns us that vain, empty words bring judgment: *"They utter mere words; with empty oaths they make covenants; so judgment springs up like poisonous weeds in the furrows of the field"* (Hosea 10:4) and *"Let no man deceive you with vain words: for because of these things cometh the wrath of God upon the children of disobedience"* (Ephesians 5:6). The negative words we confess or declare with our mouth can be a snare (net) giving the enemy *legal rights* to destroy the soul: *"A fool's mouth is his ruin, and his lips are a snare to his soul"* (Proverbs 18:7). Words can wound or fragment our soul, *"The words of a talebearer* (gossip) *are as wounds, and they go down into the innermost parts of the belly"* (Proverbs 18:8). And the multitude of words produce sin, *"In the multitude of words there wanteth not sin but he that refraineth his lips is wise"* (Proverbs 10:19).

What we declare with our mouth will either open the windows of heaven or the gates of hell. The Bible makes clear that whatever we decree by the authority of Christ, shall be, *"Thou shall also decree a thing, and it shall be established unto thee"* (Job 22:28). The Scripture declares that *"life and death are in the power of the tongue"* (Proverbs 28:21). We see evidence of the power of words throughout the Bible: God spoke the worlds into existence, *"For he spoke, and it came to be, he commanded, and it stood firm"* (Psalm 33:9). Jesus spoke only the Words of the Father, *"For I did not speak on my own, but the Father who sent me commanded me to say all that I have spoken"* (John 12:49), but He also cursed the fig tree: *"And he said to it, 'May no one ever eat fruit from you again.' And his disciples heard it"* (Mark 11:14). The next morning, the disciples *saw that the fig tree had withered away to its roots"* (Mark 11:20).

Word curses may be passed down from one generation to the next, and open doors for unclean spirits, illness, and an early death. Some common word curses are the following:

You will never amount to anything.
You are just like your father, worthless.
You are stupid.
You are ugly.
Everybody in the family has died young and you will too.
Daddy was a drunk and you will be too.
I'm sick and tired.
Everybody in the family has been divorced.
Over my dead body.
I'm just accident prone.
You're lazy.
No one loves you.
Loser.

The good news is all word curses can be broken. Scripture says, *"No weapon formed against you shall prosper and every tongue that rises against you in judgment you shall condemn"* (Isaiah 54:17). Jesus purchased our freedom from curses by becoming a curse, *"Christ purchased our freedom and redeemed us from the curse of the Law and its condemnation by becoming a curse for us—for it is written, 'Cursed is everyone who hangs (crucified) on a tree (cross)* (Galatians 3:13).

Pray this prayer:

Jesus, take your ax and break every word curse over my life. In Jesus' name, I cancel all generational curses over my life. I release the Father's blessing over my lineage. I claim the promises of Abraham, Isaac, and Jacob; I am a child of the Most High God (Psalm 82:6); I have found life and receive favor from the LORD (Proverbs 8:35). If I obey the commands of the LORD, I will be the head and not the tail, and will be on top and never at the bottom (Deuteronomy 28:13); If I follow His commandments, He will love me, bless me and multiply me according to His Word. He will also bless the fruit of my womb and the fruit of my land (Deuteronomy 7:13). The LORD has given me a crown of beauty instead of ashes, the oil of joy instead of mourning, and a garment of praise instead of a spirit of despair (Isaiah 61:1-3). The LORD has canceled all my debts, healed all my diseases, redeemed my life from destruction, crowned me with lovingkindness and tender mercies, satisfied my mouth with good things, so that my youth is renewed like the eagles' (Psalm 103:1-5). Though my father and mother forsake me, the LORD will receive me (Psalm 27:10-14). I will see the goodness of the LORD in the land of the living (Psalm 27:13). Because I have made the LORD my refuge, even the Most High, my dwelling place, no evil shall befall me, nor shall any plague come near my dwelling, for he shall give His angels charge over me, to keep me in all my ways. In their hands they shall bear me up, lest I dash my foot against a stone (Psalm 91:7-16).

Idle Words and Flattering Lips

An idle word is a *careless word* that does not align or agree with the Word of God.   Jesus said, *"But I say unto you, that every idle word that men shall speak, they shall give account thereof in the day of judgment"* (Matthew 12:36). Hence, idle words can destroy a soul, *"How long will you torment my soul, and break me in pieces with words?"* (Job 19:2). Another *soul trap or snare* of the enemy is flattery. Flattery is an excessive and insincere praise to further one's own interest or gain advantage. Flattery is a form of manipulation that feeds egos and boosts pride. Today, flattery is a means to an end, a customary practice in business and life; however, the LORD condemns it: *"The LORD shall cut off all flattering lips, [and] the tongue that speaketh proud things"* (Psalm 12:3). Flattery is a net for the soul, *"A man that flattereth his neighbor spreadeth a net for his feet"* (Proverbs 29:5 KJV).   In other words, the enemy uses flattering words to seduce and entice. Therefore, Solomon advises young people, *"Guard your heart (soul) above all else, for it determines the course of your life"* (Proverbs 4:23).

Broken Covenants or Vows

What is a covenant? A covenant is a legally binding, irreversible commitment that joins two people together. For example, marriage is a covenant or vow made between a man and a woman. God established it, so anyone who breaks the covenant of marriage, divorces, and remarries will be judged, *"And I say to you: whoever divorces his wife, except for sexual immorality, and marries another, commits adultery"* (Matthew 19:9). God hates broken covenants. For example, in Jeremiah 11:3, we see Jeremiah warning the people of Judah against breaking His covenant, *"Cursed are those who don't heed the terms of this covenant that I commanded your ancestors when I bought them out of the land of Egypt."* In Numbers 30:2, God makes it clear, *"If a man vow a vow unto the LORD or swear an oath to bind his soul with a bond; he shall not break his word, he shall do according to all that proceedeth out of his mouth."* Thus, broken vows bind the soul in captivity and lead to devastating consequences such as poverty, disaster, premature death, calamity, barrenness, and madness. Therefore, if you made a vow to the LORD, you must keep it, but if you did break it, you must repent and ask for God's mercy to release you. The LORD is merciful; we see his grace and mercy with Israel. God made a covenant with Israel, but repeatedly, the people broke their vows and pursued pagan gods. Moses interceded on their behalf, and the LORD turned from His wrath and renewed his covenant with Israel.

Adultery and Fornication

Furthermore, the soul is fragmented (broken) by fornication (sexually immoral or perverse sex) and adultery (sex outside of marriage). Solomon, the wisest man who ever lived, was led astray by his seven hundred wives and three hundred concubine including Pharaoh's daughter and women of Moab, Ammon, Edom, Sidon and of the Hittites who worshipped pagan idols. He wrote: "*Whoever commits adultery with a woman lacks understanding; He who does so destroys his own soul*" (Proverbs 6:32) Solomon warned the youth to stay away from the adulterous woman who seduces with "*fair speech*" and "*flattering lips.*" He pursues her "*Till a dart strike through his liver; as a bird hasteth to the snare, and knoweth not that it is for his life*" (Proverbs 7:23). Thus, the consequences of adultery and fornication are a fragmented (wounded) soul and death: "*For she hath cast down many wounded: yea, many strong men have been slain by her. Her house is the way to hell, going down to the chambers of death"* (Proverbs 7:26-27). In fact, those who practice such things will not inherit the Kingdom of God, *"Be not deceived: neither fornicators, nor idolaters, nor adulterers ... will inherit the Kingdom of God"* (1 Corinthians 6:9-11). Souls who divorce and remarry are violating the covenant of marriage established by God and are guilty of adultery. Today, our society approves of remarriage and blended families; in fact, it is commonplace and even acceptable in the church; however, God condemns it: *"For the LORD God of Israel says That He hates divorce, for it covers one's garment with violence," says the LORD of hosts. "Therefore, take heed to your spirit, that you do not deal treacherously"* (Malachi 2:16). The *"garment"* as mentioned in chapter 1 of *The Anatomy of the Spirit* refers to the outer wheels of the spirit. These garments can be defiled due to sin, but if you divorce, God will cover you (send) a spirit (demon) of violence or hate; therefore, you must repent of breaking your vows and the marriage covenant.

God considers marriage honorable, *"Marriage [is] honorable in all, and the bed undefiled: but the whoremongers and adulterers God will judge"* (Hebrews 13:4). Therefore, you must forgive your ex-spouse and seek reconciliation. If reconciliation is not possible, you must remain unmarried: "*A wife must not separate from her husband. But if she does, she must remain unmarried or else be reconciled to her husband. And a husband must not divorce his wife*" (1 Corinthians 7: 10-11). This, of course, goes contrary to our contemporary feel-good culture; however, *if you want to keep your soul*, you must fear God and obey His commands. God instituted the marriage covenant between one man and one woman, so God will judge the unrepentant divorced and remarried as *adulterers* or *whoremongers*. According to 1 Corinthians 6:9-11 and Revelation 21:8, adulterers and whoremongers will not inherit the Kingdom of God and will have their part in the lake of fire which is the second death. In some religions, a man can have more than one wife, but this too, violates the law of God: "*Have you not read that the one who made them at the beginning made them male and female, and said, 'For this reason a man shall leave his father and mother and be joined to his wife, and the two shall become one flesh'? So, they are no longer two, but one flesh. Therefore, what God has joined together, let no one separate*" (Matthew 19:3-6). Thus, when one divorces and remarries, he is cleaving (joining) his soul to another flesh violating God's laws. The result, the soul suffers loss and injury. This trauma invites demons of violence or hate (murder).

Soul Ties

The multitude of partners create ungodly soul ties. A soul tie is a bonding or knitting together of two souls in mind, will and emotions. Soul ties are an ungodly covenant with another person based on an unhealthy emotional and/or sexual relationship. These soul ties divide and destroy the soul. Any relationship where there is emotional dependency, manipulation, control, and confusion is unhealthy and must be broken. Soul ties with the dead such as a lost parent, child, spouse, or close friend must be broken even if it was a Godly soul tie in a healthy relationship. Unhealthy soul ties bring bondage and guilt; therefore, it is necessary to renounce it and call back every part that was given away (every emotion, will and thought that was part of the bond) and release the person by sending back all that was taken from them. Break the vows and cancel the assignments of all evil spirits sent to attempt to maintain the ungodly soul tie such as jealousy, control, confusion, co-dependency. [1] On the other hand, A healthy soul tie can bring joy and comfort. For example, David and Jonathan shared a deep bond of friendship with each other, so that *"the soul of Jonathan was knit to the soul of David, and Jonathan loved him as his own soul"* (1 Samuel 18:1).

[1] How To Minister To Specific Diseases, Healing Rooms Ministries. Spokane, Washington. 2004. Pg. 87.

Demonic Oppression and Possession

Demonic oppression and possession happen when a person's soul is captured. The soul is imprisoned in regions of darkness: *"For the enemy has pursued my soul; he has crushed my life to the ground; he has made me sit in darkness like those long dead"* (Psalm 143:3). Furthermore, the soul suffers violence, *"My soul is in the midst of lions; I lie down amid fiery beasts—the children of man, whose teeth are spears and arrows, whose tongues are sharp swords"* (Psalm 57:4) and *"Lest they tear me like a lion, Rending me in pieces, while there is none to deliver"* (Psalm 7:2). We see many examples of demonic oppression and possession in the Bible. For example, an evil spirit oppressed King Saul: *"The LORD's Spirit left Saul. Then the LORD sent an evil spirit to Saul that caused him much trouble"* (1 Samuel 16:14:23). Moreover, demons can overtake the soul. For example, in Mark 9:14-29, the father of a demon-possessed boy pleads with Jesus to heal his son: *"Teacher, I brought my son so you could heal him. He is possessed by an evil spirit that won't let him talk. And whenever this spirit seizes him, it throws him violently to the ground."* In Mark 5:1-20, Jesus healed a demon-possessed man who was overtaken by a *legion* (many) demons: *"The demons begged Jesus, 'Send us among the pigs; allow us to go into them' He gave them permission, and the impure spirits came out and went into the pigs. The herd, about two thousand in number."* In addition, sickness and disease come from demonic oppression and possession, *"And also some women who had been cured of evil spirits and diseases: Mary (called Magdalen) from whom seven demons had come out"* (Luke 8:2).

Soul Restoration

There is good news for the brokenhearted: Jesus restores the broken soul, *"He restores my soul; He leads me in the paths of righteousness For His name's sake"* (Psalm 23:3). Jesus sets the captives free, *"The Spirit of the Lord is on me, because he has anointed me to proclaim good news to the poor. He has sent me to proclaim freedom for the prisoners and recovery of sight for the blind, to set the oppressed free"* (Luke 4:18). He heals the wounded, *"He heals the brokenhearted and binds up their wounds"* (Psalm 147:3). Jesus rescues the soul from hell, *"He has redeemed my soul from going down into the pit, and my life shall look upon the light"* (Job 33:28). If you want to be set free from unhealthy soul ties, trauma, word curses, drugs, and alcohol, you must repent and submit yourself to God. For example, King David, after having an adulterous relationship with Bathsheba, the wife of Uriah the Hittite, concocts a plan to kill Uriah in battle to conceal Bathsheba's pregnancy. God sends Nathan, the prophet, to warn David, and by God's grace, David realizes, "*I have sinned against the Lord.*" David goes before the LORD in deep sorrow and longing for restoration: "*O God, according to your steadfast love; according to your abundant mercy blot out my transgressions. Wash me thoroughly from my iniquity and cleanse me from my sin! Against you, you only, have I sinned and done what is evil in your sight*" (Psalm 51:1-4). We are to humble ourselves before the LORD and ask God to restore our soul and heal our wounds. Jesus paid the price, so that we can be set free from sin, but we must be willing to acknowledge our weaknesses and failures and turn to God.

Release from Destructive Covenants, Curses, Demonic Control, Soul Bondage

This prayer is meant for those who see release and deliverance from destructive covenants, curses, demonic control, and soul bondage. The kind of covenants referred to here may be generational or entered consciously. To obtain release from such covenants, you will have to renounce them either for yourself or your ancestral line. To get rid of such deeply rooted ones, you need to pray with fervency and aggression. With this prayer, their power will be rendered null and void.

Confession:

I break ALL evil covenants, witchcraft, curses, demonic control, and soul bondages off my life and lineage in the name of the LORD JESUS CHRIST. I submit myself—body, soul and spirit to LORD JESUS, the Holy Spirit, and the Father. I make a new covenant today with the Father. The LORD has forgiven me of ALL my sins and trespasses. He has purged my iniquity:

> *"Blotting out the handwriting of ordinances that was against us, which was contrary to us, and took it out of the way, nailing it to his cross; And having spoiled principalities and powers, he made a shew of them openly, triumphing over them in it"* *(Colossians 2:14-15 NIV).*

> *"Christ hath redeemed us from the curse of the law, being made a curse for us: for it is written, cursed is everyone that hangeth on a tree: That the blessing of Abraham might come on the Gentiles through Jesus Christ; that we might receive the promise of the Spirit through faith"* *(Galatians 3:13:14).*

Prayer to Restore the Soul

Father, I ask You in the Name of Jesus Christ to send out angels to gather up the fragments of my soul and restore them to their rightful place in me (Psalm 7:2, 23:3). With the full power and authority of the Lord Jesus, I ask that angels unearth and break all earthen vessels, bonds, bands, or bindings which have been put upon my soul by any means. Restore all the pieces of my fragmented mind, will, emotions, appetite, intellect, heart, and personality. Bring them all into proper and original positions where they belong in Jesus' Name. Amen.

In the Name of Jesus Christ, I command Satan and all his demons to loosen my mind completely. I ask You, Father to send Your angels to break, cut and sever all fetters, bands, chains, ties and bonds of whatever sort the enemy has managed to place on my mind by word or deed. I ask You to loose into me and my family the spirits of the Lord: *Wisdom, Counsel, Might, Knowledge, Fear of the Lord, Power, Love, Sound Mind, Grace, Peace and the Spirit of the Lord Amen."*

Prayers taken from "Principles of Deliverance & Mass Deliverance, Booklet 27, "Pastor Win Worley, 1983, pp. 19-20

CHAPTER FOUR

The Weapons of Warfare

"For the weapons of our warfare are not carnal, but mighty through God to the pulling down of strong holds."
—2Corinthians 10:4

Today's pop culture offers fantasy to attain higher levels or worlds. We see this in many of the games that teens and young adults play. Interestingly, the games offer weapons or armor for the journey. Kids are fascinated with the types of weapons and armor to defeat the enemy. Yet, this is but a mirror of the spiritual reality, in fact, without the armor of God, we are defenseless against the enemy of our soul. In Ephesians 6:11-18 says:

"Put on the whole armor of God, that ye may be able to stand against the wiles of the devil. For we wrestle not against flesh and blood, but against principalities, against powers, against the rulers of the darkness of this world, against spiritual wickedness in high places. Wherefore take unto

you the whole armor of God, that ye may be able to withstand in the evil day, and having done all, to stand. Stand therefore, having your loins girt about with truth, and having the breastplate of righteousness; And your feet shod with the preparation of the gospel of peace. Above all, taking the shield of faith, wherewith ye shall be able to quench all the fiery darts of the wicked. And take the helmet of salvation, and the sword of the Spirit, which is the word of God: Praying always with all prayer and supplication in the Spirit and watching thereunto with all perseverance and supplication for all saints."

In the spirit realm, there are weapons of warfare against the enemy. These are the weapons we need to fight off the enemy and keep our souls. Understand that the enemy wants to destroy your soul, but you must fight to keep it. If we do not use the weapons or armor of God, we leave ourselves open and vulnerable to the attack of the enemy. For example, how do we protect ourselves from a wrathful person; the Bible teaches us in Proverbs 15:1 that *"a soft answer"* is the weapon that *"will turn away that wrath."*

The Holy Spirit

Without the Holy Spirit, you can do nothing. Jesus said, *"I am the vine, you are the branches. If you remain in me and I in you, you will bear much fruit; apart from me you can do nothing"* (John 15:5). What does that mean? It means that without Jesus, we cannot cancel curses or spells, bind, and cast out demons, heal the sick or even save our souls. We cannot depend on our own strength or wisdom to solve problems or manage the difficult circumstances of life. The seed of pride and self-righteousness produces poison fruit: sin. We must humble ourselves before God and ask Him for help. God is waiting for you to acknowledge Him as the source of life and *abundant life*. How do we receive *abundant life*? Abundant life only comes from the gift of the Holy Spirit: *"If ye then, being evil, know how to give good gifts unto your children, how much more shall your heavenly Father give the Holy Spirit to them that ask him?"* (Luke 11:23) Before Jesus ascended to heaven, he promised His disciples that he would send a helper and comforter that would guide them into all truth. Who is the Holy Spirit? He is the spirit of counsel, might, wisdom and truth. When you surrender to the Holy Spirit, the devils flee. Remember, there is a spiritual battle over our souls. When the Holy Spirit comes to live inside of you, you become a beacon of light shining in the spiritual darkness:

"Arise, shine; For your light has come! And the

glory of the Lord is risen upon you. For behold, the

darkness shall cover the earth, and deep darkness

the people; But the Lord will arise over you, and

His glory will be seen upon you "(Isaiah 60:1-3).

The presence of the Holy Spirit in our lives is our best defense against the enemy. Without His presence, we are without protection, discernment, and light. In other words, we cannot make proper decisions or choices without the discernment (wisdom) of the Holy Spirit. In Proverbs 16:9 KJV, it states that a person's heart plans his way, *"but the LORD directs his steps."* What does this mean? It means that without the Holy Spirit, we cannot even take a step lest we fall.

Power of Prayer and Tongues

To be an effective warrior, you must learn how to pray. Prayerlessness leaves us defenseless like a city without a wall. The Bible warns us about the effects of prayerlessness in Job 21:16-21:

"Lo, their good is not in their hand: the counsel of

the wicked is far from me. How oft is the candle of

the wicked put out and how oft cometh their

destruction upon them! God distributeth sorrows

> *in his anger. They are as stubble before the wind,*
> *and as chaff that the storm carrieth away. God*
> *layeth up his iniquity for his children: His eyes shall*
> *see his destruction, and he shall drink of the wrath*
> *of the Almighty. For what pleasure hath he in his*
> *house after him, when the number of his months is*
> *cut off in the midst?"*

The wicked depend on their riches and do not desire, nor seek after God; therefore, He has turned them over to punishment. As a result, the wicked lack counsel or discernment as to their lives. Lack of discernment (wisdom) leads to failure and many sorrows. The lack of prayer means lack of repentance or confession of sins, so iniquity (sin) is stored up for wrath and sudden death.

In short, those who lack relationship with God through His son, Jesus, will not inherit the kingdom of heaven. In that day, Jesus will declare to them, *"I never knew you; depart from me, you workers of lawlessness."* This may sound harsh, but this is a life-or-death race. Those who overcome through prayer and faith will have the victory. The world teaches us to be independent and self-sufficient, but we are to depend on God for everything.

Jesus showed us how to pray in Matthew 6:9-13:

"After this manner therefore pray ye: Our Father which art in heaven, Hallowed be thy name. Thy kingdom come, thy will be done on earth, as it is in heaven. Give us this day our daily bread. And forgive us our debts, as we forgive our debtors. And lead us not into temptation but deliver us from evil: For thine is the kingdom, and the power, and the glory, forever, Amen."

First, we are to recognize our position. The Father sits on His throne in majesty, glory and holiness surrounded by a host of cherubim and seraphim; the whole earth is His footstool, and we are *"but dust and our days are few and brief like grass, like flowers, blown by the wind and gone forever"* (Psalm 10314-16). In other words, when we pray, we must approach God in reverence and fear. Secondly, Jesus made the kingdom of God accessible to man through his sacrifice. We can now enter the Holy of Holies because the veil (divide) between God and mankind has been torn asunder. We have direct access to God through the blood of Jesus. Jesus bore our sins, so that we could have a relationship with our heavenly Father and creator. Thirdly, God not only meets our physical needs, but our spiritual hunger. Jesus is the hidden manna and our daily bread. Without Him, we die. He is the source of all life, so we seek His WORD to feed our spirit: *"It is written Man shall not live by bread alone, but by every word that proceedeth out of the mouth of God"* (Matthew 4:4). The WORD of God sustains the physical body as well as the spiritual body—the body and spirit are connected. Fourthly, we are to confess ALL our sins to God and forgive others. We cannot keep grudges (resentment) or unforgiveness in our hearts.

Praying in tongues is the most powerful weapon against the enemy. When you pray in tongues, you pray in an unknown language unto God: *"For he that speaketh in an [unknown] tongue speaketh not unto men, but unto God: for no man understandeth [him]; howbeit in the spirit he speaketh mysteries."* (1 Corinthians 14:2). It is a heavenly language or intimate conversation with the Father that surpasses all our understanding. It is for the spirit-filled believer a time of worship and spiritual edification. But why is it veiled in secret or mystery? Our spirit communes with the spirit of God and reveals or brings to the surface *hidden things* that are unknown to us. We are not fully made aware of it because our spiritual eyes are not open to it, but the spirit sees all things and communicates those things to the Father: *"Likewise the Spirit also helpeth our infirmities: for we know not what we should pray for as we ought, but the Spirit itself maketh intercession for us with groanings which cannot be uttered"* (Romans 8:26). This heavenly language is also hidden from the enemy. Praying in tongues opens the door to the supernatural. It is our link to heaven. When we pray earnestly in tongues, we align our spirit with the will of God, and our petitions, groanings will be heard from the throne of heaven.

The Sword of the Spirit

The Sword of the Spirit, which is the Word of God is the weapon Jesus Christ used to fight off the temptations in the wilderness: *"Take the helmet of salvation and the sword of the Spirit, which is the word of God"* (Ephesians 6:17). He quoted scripture and resisted the devil as a model for us today. When we find ourselves tempted of the Devil or even our own flesh, we must overcome by the Word of God. This by far, is one of the strongest weapons in God's arsenal. Hebrews 4:12 says, *"For the word of God is living and active, sharper than any two-edged sword, piercing to the division of soul and of spirit, of joints and of marrow, and discerning the thoughts and intentions of the heart."* Therefore, you must read and meditate on the Word daily. Psalm 1:2 says, *"But they delight in the law of the LORD, meditating on it day and night."* The Word is about Jesus himself. In John 1:1, *"In the beginning was the Word, and the Word was with God, and the Word was God."* Jesus is the Word. He is our *"daily bread,"* and we are to meditate on *His words* daily. In the spirit realm, the sword of the spirit is a mighty weapon against the enemy. We see how Jesus used the sword of the spirit, the Word of God, to resist temptation in the wilderness.

The Shield of Faith

Another weapon of the spirit is faith. In Hebrews 11:6 says that *"without faith it is impossible to please God: for he that cometh to God must believe that he is, and that he is a rewarder of them that diligently seek him."* Jesus describes faith as *"the substance of things hoped for, the evidence of things not seen."* – Hebrews 11:1. What does this mean? It means that faith is trusting in what is not seen. For example, Abraham set off to an unknown place by faith; Noah built the arc by faith; Neither Abraham nor Noah had any idea what would await them on the other side. Abraham was given no clear direction, and Noah did not know how the arc would float because he had never seen water. In fact, Noah was not given much direction as to where the arc would land.   Both men had to trust completely in God throughout the journey.

Faith is a spiritual gift given to every man: *"God hath dealt to every man the measure of faith."* – Romans 12:3. Faith is a shield against the arrows of doubt, fear and worry that rob our peace and our trust in God. God gave every man a measure of faith. Therefore, by faith, you can believe in Jesus and accept his precious gift--the salvation of your soul. Without faith, you cannot please, understand or have a relationship with the father. You must believe that He is real and accept him like a little child. *"Truly I tell you, anyone who will not receive the kingdom of God like a little child will never enter it."*—Mark 10:15.

So how does the shield of faith protect you? In Ephesians 6:16, Paul describes the function of the shield, *"Above all, taking the shield of faith, wherewith ye shall be able to quench all the fiery darts of the wicked."* In the Greek, *fiery darts* are arrows, javelins, or missiles on fire. In the spirit realm, these are real weapons the enemy uses to attack us. If your defenses are weak, or shield is down, the enemy will have the upper hand. The fiery darts come in the form of evil thoughts, attitudes, doubts, stress, sickness, selfishness, unforgiveness or strife. If we do not believe in God's Word and place our trust in His provision, the enemy will destroy us.

Helmet of Salvation and Breastplate of Righteousness

The helmet of salvation and the breastplate of righteousness are coverings for our mind and heart. The helmet protects our head, our spiritual head and breastplate protects our heart. Without the helmet, our mind (thoughts, imagination) is exposed and unprotected against the enemy. We need to repent and receive the Lord as our savior to be protected from the attacks of the enemy. The enemy speaks to your mind to deceive you, but the helmet of salvation is a covering from possession, accidental deaths, curses, and spells, but not from temptations, for even Jesus Christ was tempted of the Devil. We are saved by faith. First, we must believe or fully trust the Lord Jesus and repent of our sins to be written in the Lamb's book of life. Salvation, like faith, is a heavenly gift from a gracious Father. The breastplate of righteousness allows us to walk by faith and protects us from the deadly arrows of bitterness, unforgiveness and hate. We are to have a clean heart and an upright spirit:

> *"I will sprinkle clean water on you, and you shall be clean from all your uncleanness, and from all your idols I will cleanse you. And I will give you a new heart, and a new spirit I will put within you. And I will remove the heart of tone from your flesh and give you a heart of flesh. And I will put my Spirit within you and cause you to walk in my statutes and be careful to obey my rules." – Ezekiel 36:25-27*

It is in the heart of our spirit where the *Holy Spirit* comes to live and abide. The Kingdom of Heaven is within you in your heart.

(Luke 17:21) It is there, the fountain of life. *"For with thee is the fountain of life: in thy light shall we see light."* (Psalm 36:9). This is a picture of the holy of holies or the inner sanctuary of the Tabernacle where God's presence appeared over the Ark of the Covenant, the Mercy Seat (Exodus 26:34). It was the place where blood was sprinkled on the Mercy Seat or over the top of the Ark as an atonement for the sins of Israel. (Leviticus 16:15). The only people allowed to enter the Holy of Holies was the High priest. There was only one high priest at a time, and he could enter only once a year. Today, the High priest is Jesus Christ who enters our heart or holy of holies. He sprinkles our heart with his blood and cleans us from all our iniquity and gives us a breastplate of righteousness.

How do we put on the armor of God? We put it on by seeking the Kingdom of God and His righteousness above everything else (Matthew 6:33). We must allow the sword of the spirit or the Word to penetrate our heart and cleanse us from all unrighteousness. We must be conformed to the image of Christ (Romans 8:29) and die to ourselves. When we tolerate sin, refuse to forgive, worry, or do not develop an intimate relationship with God, we take off the breastplate leaving ourselves vulnerable to attack.

We use the armor to live a victorious life by *"Destroying speculations and every lofty thing raised up against the knowledge of God and we are taking every thought captive to the obedience of Christ."* –2 Corinthians 10:15. Every thought that enters your brain is not your own. The armor is necessary for protecting us from evil thoughts, suggestions, and ideas that the enemy tries to plant in your mind. For example, the enemy might plant in your mind that your parents do not really care about you. This in turn, will not only devastate you, but destroy you. If you nurture or meditate on the words of the enemy, the seeds of hatred, division and strife will begin to grow and you will begin to isolate yourself from your family, resent their counsel and distrust them. You will eventually bear fruit by dishonoring and disobeying them violating God's laws to honor your parents. This in turn will lead to further oppression such as depression, suicidal thoughts, and violence. The enemy is real, too. In John 10:10, Jesus says, *"the thief cometh not, but that he may steal, and kill, and destroy; I came that they may have life and may have it abundantly."* We are at war with a powerful enemy, so let us put on the armor of God and fight.

Garments of Salvation and Robe of Righteousness

Isaiah 61:10 KJV speaks of being clothed in a *garment of salvation* and covered with the *robe of righteousness*. These are spiritual garments or coverings we receive at our salvation. Before salvation, our spirit body was covered in a *veil of darkness or polluted garments*: "*But the people's minds were hardened, and to this day whenever the old covenant is being read, the same veil covers their minds so they cannot understand the truth. And this veil can be removed only by believing in Christ*" (2 Corinthians 3:14) and our understanding was darkened: "*Having the understanding darkened, being alienated from the life of God through the ignorance that is in them, because of the blindness of their heart*" (Ephesians 4:18) but after receiving the gift of salvation, we were restored to a right relationship with the father, so we were given a robe of righteousness, not of self-righteousness or good works, but the Lord's righteousness and covering over our lives.

Oil of Joy and Garment of Praise

Isaiah 61:3 prophesizes the coming of the Messiah and the work He will do: "*To appoint unto them that mourn in Zion, to give unto them beauty for ashes, the oil of joy for mourning, the garment of praise for the spirit of heaviness; that they might be called trees of righteousness, the planting of the LORD, that he might be glorified.*" One of the greatest weapons that the enemy uses against the believer is discouragement, or the *spirit of heaviness*, so we must put on the garment of praise or offer a sacrifice of praise despite our circumstances or feelings. In the natural, it may seem unusual to offer praise during times of trouble or sorrow, but in the invisible realm, offering praise to God lifts the spirit of oppression or heaviness and restores the soul. For example, we see this in the life of David who faced great discouragement. In Psalm 13:1-6, David cries out to the Lord,

> *"How long wilt thou forget me, O LORD? How long wilt thou hide thy face from me? How long shall I take counsel in my soul, having sorrow in my heart daily? How long shall mine enemy be exalted over me? Consider and hear me, O LORD my God: lighten mine eyes, lest I sleep the sleep of death; Lest mine enemy say, I have prevailed against him; and those that trouble me rejoice when I am moved. But I have trusted in thy mercy; my heart shall rejoice in thy salvation. I will sing unto the LORD because he hath dealt bountifully with me."*

Notice that the schemes or plans of the enemy have not changed for over three thousand years. The enemy wants to make you feel abandoned and forgotten by God, but David prays and encourages himself in the LORD despite his feelings or circumstances. In 2 Chronicles 20:20-24, we see that King Jehoshaphat received a revelation in the spirit about the garment of praise when he appointed singers to praise and give thanks to the LORD before their enemies, and *"when they began singing and praising, the LORD set ambushes against the sons of Ammon, Moab and Mount Seir, who had come against Judah."* If you want the Lord to set traps for your enemy or (rulers of darkness), sing and praise Him.

Power in the Name of The Lord

In 1 Samuel 17:45, David declares to the Philistine giant, *"You come to me with a sword, a spear and a javelin, but I come to you in the name of the LORD of hosts, the God of the armies of Israel, whom you have taunted."* The Lord of hosts is the commander of the angelic armies. David received a revelation of the future Messiah and King. In Psalm 24:10, David confirms the identity of the *LORD of hosts*, *"Who is this King of glory? The LORD of hosts, he is the King of glory."* The name of the LORD is the most powerful weapon in the universe, so *"that at the name of Jesus every knee should bow, of those in heaven, and of those on earth, and of those under the earth, and that every tongue should confess that Jesus Christ is Lord, to the glory of God the Father."* (Philippians 2:10-11) What does this mean? It means that all spiritual wickedness in high places, on earth and even under the earth (hell) will have to bow before the name. In Romans 10:13, Paul writes, *"For whosoever shall call upon the*

[85]

name of the Lord shall be saved." The name of Jesus has power not only over the visible and invisible worlds, but power over death and destruction (Hades).

Power in the Blood of Christ

The blood of Jesus is equivalent to a hydrogen bomb in the spirit realm and a formidable weapon in the Christian's arsenal. According to Revelation 12: 11, *"And they overcame him (Satan) by the blood of the Lamb..."* In other words, His blood gives us power over the enemy. The shed blood of Jesus made atonement for our sins and restored our souls. It is only through the blood that we are cleansed from all iniquity: *"the blood of Jesus Christ His Son cleanses us from all sin."* (1 John 1:7) The blood of Jesus also made it possible to have fellowship with God. According to Ephesians 2:13, *"But now in Christ Jesus you who once were far away have been brought near through the blood of Christ."*

Power Over the Works of the Devil

There is a mystery surrounding the wounds of Christ, but the wounds were necessary for healing our souls from curses and destroying the works of the enemy. According to Galatians 3:13,

"Christ redeemed us from the curse of the law by becoming a curse for us. "It was necessary for Jesus to become a curse for us to free us from the curse of Adam. The curse infected all creation and the earth. Through Jesus' wounds we are not only set free from the law of sin and death, but we are healed of all curses and diseases. According to Isaiah 53:5, Isaiah declares that our Savior was "wounded (pierced through) for our transgressions, bruised (crushed) for our iniquities and by His stripes (blows that cut in) we are healed. Through Jesus' wounds, we are set free from Satan's authority. Jesus destroyed the works of the Devil through his sacrifice, *"For this purpose the Son of God was manifested, that He might destroy the works of the devil"* (1 John 3:8). Hence, we have power over the enemy through Christ.

Dominion

Thorns in the Bible are always associated with the curse of barrenness upon the land as a byproduct of sin. In the Genesis 3:18, one of the curses brought on by Adam and Eve's disobedience was *thorns and thistles* upon the land: *"Thorns also and thistles shall it bring forth to thee; and thou shalt eat the herb of the field."* The land would be cursed and produce thorns and thistles instead of yielding its fruit. In other words, Adam and Eve's sin allowed Satan to have dominion over the whole Earth, but the shed blood of Jesus from the crown of thorns removed the curse of barrenness over the land and reestablished God's kingdom or dominion upon the Earth. Hence, the children of God now have authority on Earth to take back the *waste places or dominions of darkness and* tear down strongholds. Romans 6:14 states: *"For sin shall not have dominion over you: for ye are not under the law, but under grace"* and Luke 10:19, *"Behold, I give you the authority to trample on serpents and scorpions, and over all the power of the enemy, and nothing shall by any means hurt you."* The LORD wants us to break up the *fallow* (hard, dry) *ground* overgrown with thorns and thistles, so that it might become fruitful: *"Sow to yourselves in righteousness, reap in mercy; break up your fallow ground; for it is time to seek the LORD, till he come and rain righteousness upon you."* (Hosea 10:12) The ground is men's souls (heart), and the thorns represent the cares of this life *"He also that received seed among the thorns is he that heareth the word; and the care of this world and deceitfulness of riches, choke the word, and he becometh unfruitful."* (Matthew 13:22)

Therefore, Jesus came to set us free from the curse of sin that chokes the seed. In Psalms 55:22, David says, *"Cast your cares on the LORD and he will sustain you; he will never let the righteous fall."* Sin is a failure to trust God and His goodness, so we must humble ourselves before God and cast all our cares on

Him. Sin makes men unproductive, unfruitful, and vulnerable to the attacks of the enemy. *"Humble yourselves, therefore, under God's mighty hand, that he may lift you up in due time. Cast all your anxiety on him because he cares for you. Be self-controlled and alert. Your enemy the devil prowls around like a roaring lion looking for someone to devour"* (1 Peter 5:6-8) We are to live our lives dependent on His provision to meet all our needs: *"But seek ye first his kingdom, and his righteousness; and all these things shall be added unto you"* (Matthew 6:33) .

Power to Tear Down Strongholds

A stronghold is a pattern of thinking rooted in deception. Strongholds are built when we accept and meditate on lies. It forms in our minds' imagination, a false concept that we believe to be true, but is not. For example, if you believe God is angry with you, this is a false perception or stronghold because it will prevent you from having a relationship with the Father. The enemy will continue to build and fortify this stronghold in your mind. He will bring more devils to the strong tower such as fear, depression, anxiety into your life to sever your trust and faith in God.

How do we take down strongholds over our lives? 2 Corinthians 10:4, "For *the weapons of our warfare are not carnal, but mighty through God to the pulling down of strongholds; casting down imaginations, and every high thing that exalteth itself against the knowledge of God and bringing into captivity every thought to the obedience of Christ."* Imaginations must be cast down through the renewing of our minds: *"And be not conformed to this world: but be ye transformed by the renewing of your mind, that ye may prove what is that good, and acceptable, and perfect, will of God"* (Romans 12:2). As our minds are renewed, we prove what is good, acceptable and the perfect will of God. It is through the washing of the Word that our minds are transformed, and strongholds are torn down. Spending time and meditating on Jesus and His Word, God washes our minds and corrects our false thinking patterns: *"That he might sanctify and cleanse it with the washing of water by the word, That he might present it to himself a glorious church, not having spot, or wrinkle, or any such thing; but that it should be holy and without blemish"* (Ephesians 5:26-27).

Power Over Sickness and Death

In the Old Testament, one of the punishments for wickedness was receiving stripes or whips made of braided leather with pottery shards and sharp stones, which tore open the flesh of the prisoner. In addition to the physical agony, he endured the humiliation of punishment. In Deuteronomy 25:2,

"And it shall be if the wicked man has deserved to be beaten, that the judge shall cause him to lie down, and be beaten before his face, according to the measure of his wickedness with a certain number of stripes." The only corporal punishment named in the Torah was that of stripes. The culprit was to be beaten in the presence of the judges and the stripes could not exceed forty lashes. (Deuteronomy 25:2,3) In the New Testament, (2 Corinthians 11:24), no more than thirty-nine stripes were administered in multiples of three-two stripes on the back and one on the breast. The *stripes on the back* represent judgment, punishment, or curses. For example, King Solomon talks about the punishment or judgment of a fool: "Judgments are prepared for scorners, and stripes for the back of fools" (Proverbs 19:29), and *"A whip for the horse, a bridle for the ass, and a rod for the fool's back"* (Proverbs 26: 3). Jesus gave his back or paid the penalty for our foolish conduct and mistakes. The *stripes on his backside* also represent the punishment of sickness and death; the LORD endured the scourging to free us from sickness and spiritual death. For example, on his sickbed, Hezekiah king of Judah prayed to be delivered from his sickness and pleaded with the LORD, *"but thou hast in love to my soul delivered it from the pit of corruption: for thou hast cast all my sins behind thy back"* (Isaiah 38:17).

Jesus cast all our sins on his back to heal all our infirmities and pay the wages of sin. The Prophet Isaiah prophesizes that the Messiah would give his backside to the tormentors or punishers (Isaiah 50:5). Do you understand what this means? Jesus offered up his body to be tortured, flogged, and crucified as payment for our sins. God said that he would *visit transgression (sin) with the rod, and iniquity with stripes* (Psalm 89:32). The *stripes on his back* heal and restore our souls. The Messiah would be *"wounded for our transgressions, bruised for our iniquities: the chastisement of our peace was upon him; and with his stripes we are healed"* (Isaiah 53:5). In other words, *by his stripes*, we were healed and made whole. The healing of the inner man precedes the healing of the outer man (body). It was the shedding of His sinless blood (life) by flogging that we are restored and delivered from the consequences of sin and death.

Power over Sin

The Jewish prophet, Zechariah points to a future event where Jews *"will look on the one they have pierced"* and mourn because of him (Zechariah 12:10). In Revelations 1:7, John writes about the second coming of the Messiah: *"Look, he is coming with the clouds, and every eye will see him, even those who pierced him; and all the peoples of the earth will mourn because of him"* Crucifixion, probably originating with the Babylonians and Assyrians, was one of the most brutal and shameful ways to die. Death resulted in either *hypovolemic shock* due to prolonged rapid heartbeat or the buildup of fluid around the heart. In either case, the soldier needed to confirm Jesus was dead, so they shoved a spear into His side, through the rib cage, rupturing the pericardial sack resulting in a flow of both blood and water. What does all this mean? Jesus was pierced for our transgressions or sins, so that we would have dominion over sin. Romans 6:14-23 says, *"For sin shall not have dominion over you: for ye are not under the law, but under grace."* In other words, we are no longer slaves to sin: *"Now you are free from your slavery to sin, and you have become slaves to righteous living"* (Romans 6:18). We have the power to resist and renounce sin in our lives.

Power to Forgive

How can Satan hold our soul in captivity? There are traps set by the enemy, but lack of forgiveness is a sin that holds us in bondage and cuts off our relationship with the father. In Matthew 5:22-24 Jesus warns that *"Everyone who is angry with his brother will be liable to judgment; whoever insults his brother will be liable to the council; and whoever says, 'You fool!' will be liable to the hell of fire."* Unforgiveness and anger will lead you straight to hell. If someone molested, betrayed, or abused you in

[93]

any way, we are commanded to forgive—no matter what. The abuse may have been severe and prolonged, but you must not allow the seed of bitterness to take root and destroy you because this is the plan of the enemy. How do we forgive our enemies? Let us take the example of Jesus on the cross. The soldiers were dividing up his clothes and casting lots and Jesus said, "*Father forgive them, for they do not know what they are doing.*" (Luke 23:24). Jesus knows that the real enemy of our souls are not people, but demonic entities, principalities of darkness. In Ephesians 6:12, Paul writes, "*For we wrestle not against flesh and blood, but against principalities, against powers, against the rulers of the darkness of this world, against spiritual wickedness in high places.*" In other words, we are not struggling with mere mortals here, we are battling dark forces from another dimension. These ancient aliens have been around since the beginning of creation. To resist the real enemy, we must understand how the kingdom of darkness operates. The good news is that we are not left defenseless. We have a powerful tool: the power to forgive.

We can come to God, repent, or confess our unforgiveness, and he will not only forgive us, but cleanse us from ALL unrighteousness. 1 John 1:9 says, "*If we confess our sins, he is faithful and just and will forgive us our sins and purify us from all unrighteousness.*" The Jews had to bring sin offerings to the temple on a regular basis to atone (pay) for their sins, but under the new covenant, we are restored (forgiven) through Jesus' sacrifice. Peter asked how many times I shall forgive my brother, and Jesus answered, "*I tell you, not seven times, but seventy-seven times*" (Matthew 18:22). *Seventy-seven times* means that we must forgive others as many times as needed. If we are to imitate Jesus, we must walk in the fruits of the spirit: love, self-control, meekness, patience, faithfulness, joy, long-suffering, and temperance. Long-suffering means showing great love and patience despite suffering or persecution, "*so that the proven character of your faith—more valuable than gold which, though perishable, is refined by fire—may result in praise, glory and honor at the revelation of Jesus Christ*" (1 Peter 1:7).

Power Over All the Enemy

King David was blessed to have a close walk with God, so God opened his eyes to see into the spiritual realm. David had many close encounters with *principalities, powers, rulers of darkness and spiritual wickedness*, that he overcame through ardent prayer and the grace of God. For example, David writes,

> "*The sorrows of hell compassed me about: the snares of death prevented me. In my distress I*

> *called upon the Lord and cried unto my God: he*
> *heard my voice out of his temple, and my cry came*
> *before him even into his ears." (Psalms 17:13)*

> *"For thou wilt not leave my soul in hell: neither wilt*
> *thou suffer thine Holy One to see corruption."*
> *(Psalms 16:10)*

> *"He delivered me from my strong enemy, and from*
> *them which hated me: for they were too strong for*
> *me." (Psalms 18:17)*

The beasts mentioned are not physical beasts, but other worldly dark forces operating in the spirit realm. It is important that you understand that these dark forces are real; they are continually waging war with the saints and God's angelic hosts. For example, in the Book of Daniel 10:13, we see that the Prophet Daniel prayed and fasted 21 days, and the LORD appeared to him saying:

> *"Fear not, Daniel: for from the first day that thou*
> *didst set thine heart to understand, and to chasten*
> *thyself before thy God, thy words were heard, and*
> *I come for thy words. But the prince of the*
> *kingdom of Persia withstood me one and twenty*
> *days: but lo, Michael, one of the chief princes,*

came to help me; and I remained there with the
kings of Persia."

The prince of the kingdom of Persia is a fallen angel, ruler of a region. According to this passage, they were waging war in the heavens, and Michael, an archangel, battled this entity. Why do we need to understand this? It is important that your *eyes of understanding* are opened to the truth. We are at war with a real enemy, not of flesh and blood, but of a well-organized army of fallen angels and demon hordes.

However, we have power over these dark rulers. In fact, we were given authority over these powers: "*I have given you authority to trample on snakes and scorpions and to overcome ALL the power of the enemy; nothing will harm you*" (Luke 10:19). Do you understand what this means? Jesus grants us power over these rulers to take back dominion and establish the Kingdom of God on Earth. We are to advance the Kingdom of God to ALL the earth by force: "*From the days of John the Baptist until now, the kingdom of heaven has been suffering violence, and the violent have been seizing it by force*" (Matthew 11:12). According to Thayer's Greek lexicon, *the violent* refers to the strong or forceful who strive to obtain the privileges with the utmost eagerness and effort. In other words, there is a war between the forces of evil and good to establish the Kingdom of God on Earth.

King David wrestled with demon principalities during his lifetime. These devils are rulers of darkness assigned over states, regions, nations of the world.

Authority Over the Earth

It is important to know that devils govern over regions and nations. These spirits have entered blood covenants with worldly rulers, warlocks, and witches to legally seize territories and bring hell on earth. There are two kingdoms at war in the spiritual realm: The Kingdom of Heaven and the realm of hell. Both kingdoms are fighting for dominion, but they legally need the permission of *man* to establish reign on Earth. In Genesis 1:26, God established man as the ruler of the Earth: "*Then God said, 'Let us make man in our image, after our likeness. And let them have dominion over the fish of the sea and over the birds of the heavens and over the livestock and over all the earth.*" But after the fall of Adam, the devil seized control of all the kingdoms of the Earth. As evidenced in Luke 4:6, Jesus was taken up to a high mountain and shown all the kingdoms of the world, and the devil said, "*To you I will give all this authority and their glory, for it has been delivered to me, and I give it to whom I will.*" However, Jesus' sacrifice not only redeemed man, but purchased his authority: "*I have given you authority to trample on snakes and scorpions and to overcome all the power of the enemy*" (Luke

10:19). *Snakes and scorpions* as mentioned in Psalms 91 are types of devils. Therefore, we have victory in Jesus Christ to take back the Earth. Jesus promises, *"Blessed are the meek (humble): for they shall inherit the earth"* (Matthew 5:5).

Hence, our mission as power-filled believers is to do the will of the Father--establish the Kingdom of Heaven on earth: *"Your kingdom come, your will be done, on earth as it is in heaven"* (Matthew 6:10). But how do we establish God's kingdom on earth? We take the Kingdom of Heaven by force: *"From the days of John the Baptist until now, the kingdom of heaven has been subjected to violence, and violent people have been raiding it"* (Matthew 11:12). This means that there is a spiritual battle going on between the *violent people* (God's people) and the *forces of darkness in the second heaven*. God's people overcome the enemy and take authority through prayer and fasting.

The Power to Pull Down Strongholds

The Holy Spirit empowers you to *pull down strongholds, cast down imaginations and bring into captivity every thought to the obedience of Christ* (2 Corinthians 10:4-5). What are strongholds? Strongholds are addictions, negative attitudes, and habits that we have permitted in our lives; Ephesians 4:27 *"and*

[99]

do not give the devil a foothold" means to not give the devil an opportunity to work or a place in our lives. In other words, every time we sin, it gives Satan the legal right to reign and rule over us. Unrepentant sin festers the heart and mind. It becomes a strong tower that must be torn down if we are to grow in Christ. The stronghold enters as a thought, grows, and takes root in our heart, consuming our mind and imagination. For example, pornography is a common stronghold for many men and women today, and pornographic images are everywhere in our society; the internet has made this insidious evil more accessible than ever; In fact, child pornography has become one of the most solicited forms of pornography on the dark web; It is a multi-billion dollar industry in our society. Gaming is another stronghold. Kids spend 6 to 8 hours a day playing games on their phones or devices while neglecting relationships and responsibilities. In short, any distraction or sin that overpowers us is a stronghold.

So how do we *"pull down strongholds,"* and *"cast down imaginations"* and *"bring every thought to the obedience of Christ?"* We cannot do it on our own strength, so we must humble ourselves before an almighty God, confess our sins and repent. True repentance means to stop sinning. After you have stopped, you must ask God to erase and clean your soul and mind of all images, addictions and to strengthen your inner man. You must also ask the LORD to restore your soul and deliver you from any demonic power or ruler in your life. Ask the elders of your church to pray over you and speak deliverance. In 2 Corinthians 10:4, *"For the weapons of our warfare are not fleshly, but divinely powerful toward the demolition of strongholds."* If we cry out to the Lord, he will give us the power to overcome the forces of hell and be victorious. Even in our dream state, the Lord has the power to shut down unclean thoughts, dreams, and images from our mind.

We must shut out sin from our eyes, ears and mouth and ask the LORD to" create *a clean heart"* and *"renew a right spirit within us"* (Psalm 51:10). This means that we must renew our minds daily with the Word and ask the Holy Spirit to help us in our walk, but if you are not saved, you must first believe that Jesus died on the cross and paid the penalty for your sins, *"For God so loved the world, that he gave his only begotten Son, that whosoever believeth in him should not perish, but have everlasting life."* (John 3:16); God's love for us is so great that he is willing to remove our sins *"as far as the east is from the west, so far has he removed our transgressions from us"* (Psalm 103:12). God promises to wipe the slate clean, *"For I will forgive their iniquities and will remember their sins no more*" (Hebrews 8:12).

The Power to See in the Spirit

King David understood that his enemies were not flesh and blood, but strong forces from the pit of hell bent on destroying his soul. King David's spiritual eyes were opened to see these dark forces oppressing him, and in the *Book of Psalms*, we read how he pleaded with God to rescue his soul from these strong enemies.

Everyone has both physical eyes to see the material world, and spiritual eyes to see in the spirit realm; however, unless God opens your *spiritual eyes*, you will remain unaware of the spiritual warfare going on all around you. For example, in 2 Kings 6:9-17, we read the account of Israel facing certain annihilation from the Syrians, but Elisha, the Prophet, warned the King of Israel of the approaching army, and as a result, the Syrian army surrounded Elisha's camp with horses and chariots. When Elisha's servant saw the great army, he cried out to the Prophet, '*Alas, my master! What shall we do*?' and Elisha prayed and said, "*LORD, I pray, open his eyes that he may see. Then the LORD opened the eyes of the servant and he saw a mountain full of horses and chariots of fire all around Elisha.*" We need to pray like Elisha that the LORD opens our *spiritual eyes* to see the real battle.   Another example of spiritual eyes opening is found in Numbers 22, where Balak, King of the Moabites, summoned the prophet and sorcerer Balaam to curse Israel, and as Balaam saddled his donkey and went to curse Israel, the Angel of the LORD stood with drawn sword in His hand blocking Balaam's path, *"then the LORD opened Balaam's eyes, and he saw the Angel standing in the way, and he bowed his head and fell flat on his face."*

The Power of Prophetic Vision

In the New Testament, the Apostle Paul writes, *"The god of this age has blinded the minds of unbelievers, so that they cannot see the light of the gospel that displays the glory of Christ, who is the image of God"* (2 Corinthians 4:4). The enemy causes *spiritual blindness*, so that souls remain in darkness; however, Jesus said, *"I am the light of the world: he that followeth me shall not walk in darkness but shall have the light of life"* (John 8:12). Jesus came to give sight to the blind—to open their *eyes of understanding*. Paul refers to the *eyes of understanding* being enlightened, *"The eyes of your understanding being enlightened; that ye may know what the hope of his calling is, and what the riches of the glory of his inheritance in the saints"* (Ephesians 1:18). In other words, Jesus reveals His will and purpose for your life, so that you are no longer stumbling around in the darkness concerning your life and calling.

The *eyes of your understanding being enlightened* is a powerful weapon against the forces of darkness because once you know who you are in Christ, then *"no weapon formed against you will prosper"* (Isaiah 54:17). Once you understand *the hope of his calling for your life, the riches of the glory, the exceeding greatness of his power,* you will walk in supernatural boldness and power. Pray that your eyes will be opened.

Power Over Death

Jesus Christ defeated the *spirit of death* and gave us power over it: *"O death, where is your victory? O death, where is your sting? For sin is the sting that results in death, and the law gives sin its power. But thank God! He gives us victory over sin and death through our Lord Jesus Christ"* (1 Corinthians 15:55-57). As born-again believers, we have the *dunamis* (dynamite) power to raise the dead. The Greek word *dunamis* in the Bible means "power, force or ability." This power is available to us through the Holy Spirit: *"You will receive power when the Holy Spirit has come upon you"* (Acts 1:8). Dunamis is used over one hundred times in the New Testament to describe the explosive (resurrection) power of God, *"I am the resurrection and the life.*

Whoever believes in me, though he die, yet shall he live" (John 11:25). Therefore, we can boldly renounce the *spirit of death* and declare life over ourselves: "*I shall not die, but live, and declare the works of the LORD*" (Psalm 118:17).

Powers of God

From the beginning, God has anointed men (prophets) with supernatural powers and abilities to accomplish his purpose. For example, God selected Moses to lead his people out of Egypt through signs and wonders. He chose the prophet Elijah to warn a nation by commanding nature and pronouncing judgement. Finally, He chose Jesus to redeem mankind, bring salvation to the world through creative miracles and resurrection power. Hence, God's powers are manifested to bring mankind to repentance and reconciliation. Therefore, as disciples and servants of God, we have access to these powers through the Holy Spirit. Jesus performed *the works* that the Father had given him to accomplish. Throughout Jesus ministry, these *works* included raising the dead, multiplying food, commanding the wind and the waves, walking on water and tele porting; however, Jesus told his disciples, "*Truly, truly, I say to you, whoever believes in me will also do the works that I do, and greater works than these will he do, because I am going to the Father*" (John

14:12). Therefore, as believers, we are to do the *works* that Jesus did and more.

Prayer of Repentance and Protection over your School, Community, City and Nation

Father, we humble ourselves before you. We acknowledge our sins before you: sins of idolatry, bigotry, violence, cruelty, rebellion, pride, vanity, immorality, apathy, whoredom, sloth, injustice, murder, ignorance; We have abandoned you. We have followed other gods, served them, and bowed in worship to them (Jeremiah 16:11). We have not followed your instructions or obeyed your commands. Our sins are not concealed from you, and our iniquity is not hidden from your sight (Jeremiah 16:17). You said in your word, that if a people about which I have made the announcement turns from its evil, I will relent concerning the disaster I had planned to do it (Jeremiah 18:8). Do not bring harm to this place, for we turn from our evil ways, stubbornness, and evil heart (Jeremiah 18:12). You say, "If my people which are called by my name, shall humble themselves, and pray, and seek my face, and turn from their wicked ways; then will I hear from heaven, and will forgive their sin, and will heal their land" (2 Chronicles 7:14). Have mercy upon us, O God, according to thy loving kindness: according unto the multitude of thy tender mercies blot out our transgressions.

Wash us thoroughly from our iniquity and cleanse us from sin. For we acknowledge our transgressions: and our sin is ever before us (Psalm 51:1-4). Deliver us from our enemies, O God: defend us from those that rise up against us. Deliver us from the workers of iniquity and save us from bloody men (Psalm 59:1-2). For though we walk in the flesh, we do not war according to the flesh. For the weapons of our warfare are not carnal but mighty in God for pulling down strongholds, casting down arguments and every high thing that exalts itself against the knowledge of God, bringing every though into captivity to the obedience of Christ (2 Corinthians 10:3-5) and no weapon formed against us shall prosper, and every tongue that shall rise against us in judgment thou shalt condemn" (Isaiah 54:17). For they intended evil against us: they imagined a mischievous device, which they are not able to perform. Therefore, shalt thou make them turn their back when thou shalt make ready thine arrows upon thy strings against the face of them. Be thou exalted, LORD, in thine own strength: so, will we sing and praise thy power (Psalm 21:12).

Prayer of Spiritual Warfare Against the Enemy

For whom is God save the LORD? Or who is a rock save our God? It is God that girdeth me with strength, and maketh my way perfect. He maketh my feet like hinds' feet, and setteth me upon my high places. He teacheth my hands to war, so that a bow of steel is broken by mine arms. Thou hast also given me the shield of thy salvation: and thy right hand hath holden me up, and thy gentleness hath made me great. Thou hast enlarged my steps under me, that my feet did not slip. I have pursued mine enemies and overtaken them: neither did I turn again till they were consumed. I have wounded them that they were not able to rise they are fallen under my feet. For thou hast girded me with strength unto the battle: thou hast subdued under me those that revolted against me. Thou hast also given me the necks of mine enemies: that I might destroy them that hate me (Psalm 18:31-40). For you, LORD, have delivered me from death, my eyes from tears, my feet from stumbling (Psalm 116:8). I will praise you, O Lord my God, with all my heart; I will glorify Your name" (Psalm 86:12). Lift up your heads, O gates! And be lifted up, O ancient doors, that the King of glory may come in. Who is this King of glory? The LORD of hosts. The LORD, strong and mighty, the LORD, mighty in battle! (Psalm 24: 7-10).

CHAPTER FIVE

The Dangers of Magic, Sorcery, Divination and Astrology

"For what will it profit a man if he gains the whole world and loses his own soul? Or what will a man give in exchange for his soul? –Matthew 16:26 NKJV

In 2001, the author J.K. Rowling released *Harry Potter and the Sorcerer's Stone,* the book was a great success worldwide that led to a series of books and films. Children around the world were reading about Harry's adventures in the world of wizardry, awakening an appetite for the occult. Incidentally, the sorcerer's stone or philosopher's stone is a much sought-after item in the occult and black-magic world. In fact, the third floor of HOGWARTS is forbidden to all except those who are selected to have this knowledge and access. J.K. Rowling's Harry Potter series introduced an entire generation to witchcraft, sorcery, and magic. This also opened a door to occult or hidden knowledge. God is not against knowledge itself, but the lusting after secret knowledge that God has not chosen to reveal, "*The secret things belong to the Lord our God, but the things revealed belong to us and to our sons forever*" (Deuteronomy 29:29 NKJV).

This quest for hidden knowledge was embedded in man from the time The Watchers (Sons of God) led a rebellion against God, descended on Mt. Hermon, took wives from among the daughters of men and began to breed a hybrid race of giants upon the earth called the Nephilim (Genesis 6:1-4) According to the Book of Enoch, the Watchers revealed occult secrets to mankind teaching them the art of cosmetics, metallurgy, medicine, astrology, enchantments and root-cuttings, agriculture and war (The Book of Enoch Ch. 8:1-2). As a result of this secret knowledge, there was great lawlessness, unrighteousness upon the earth, and men began to perish from off the face of the earth. Likewise, this secret knowledge is increasing today. According to Daniel 12:4, "*But thou, O Daniel, shut up the words, and seal the book, even to the time of the end: many shall run to and fro, and knowledge shall be increased.*" In this verse, the word *knowledge* means *knowledge of God, understanding or wisdom,* but God declares the end from the beginning, so makes it clear that both the knowledge of good and evil shall increase such as in the days of Noah.

So how has this knowledge increased? We have seen a rapid spiraling of advances in technology, science, medicine, and information with serious side effects. For example, scientists can now edit the DNA of fetuses in the womb, gene splice human, animal and plant DNA creating hybrid crops and animals, produce deadly bioweapons and vaccines in a laboratory and develop nanotechnology capable of providing cheap renewable energy while posing serious risks to the environment and human health. As a society, we are essentially rebelling against God's perfect design and creating our own monster race--replacing God's image with our own.

Magick

The word magic comes from the Latin magicus or from the Persian Magi. The "k" in Magick was adopted by Aleister Crowley, a 20th century occultist. According to Crowley, Magick is *"the science and art of causing change to occur in conformity with the Will."* Crowley authored *The Book of the Law* that expounds his most famous teaching, *"Do what thou wilt shall be the whole of the law."* After his death, Crowley's teachings became a mantra for celebrities and popular culture. In 1 Samuel 15:23, *"For rebellion is as the sin of witchcraft and stubbornness is as iniquity and idolatry."* At the heart of the practice of witchcraft and sorcery is rebellion and stubbornness brought on by self-will. God gave mankind free will to choose, but he chose the tree of the knowledge of good and evil instead of the tree of life.

The Bible warns us about divination, sorcery, and magic. In fact, God strictly forbids people to practice these things: *"Do not practice divination or sorcery."* (Leviticus 19:26) But what are the consequences of such practices? Many young people, including Christians, think it is harmless fun to engage in occult practices such as reading the horoscope, talking to the dead or reading natal or astrological charts. However, God clearly warns His people not to look to mediums, fortune tellers or signs for guidance, direction, and purpose but the Word of God. The Israelites, for example, despite their direct contact with the God of the universe, turned away from God to practice these things and the LORD warned them:

> *"When you enter the land the LORD your God is giving you, do not learn to imitate the detestable ways of the nations there. Let no one be found among you who sacrifices his son or daughter in the fire (infanticide), who practices divination or sorcery, interprets omens, engages in witchcrafts, or casts spells, or who is a medium or who consults the dead. Anyone who does these things*

is detestable to the LORD, and because of these

detestable practices the LORD your God will drive

out those nations before you. You must be

blameless before the LORD your God. The nations

you will dispossess listen to those who practice

sorcery or divination. But as for you, the LORD your God

has not permitted you to do so." (Deuteronomy 18:9-14)

Spirit of Abortion and Infanticide

God detested these practices because it meant that the Israelites broke covenant with God and gave heed to seducing spirits and demons. They became defiled because they *imitated* the practices of pagan nations and sought-after pagan gods. In Psalm 106:34-39, God details the sins of the Israelites for not destroying the pagan nations, but intermingling (merging) with them, serving their idols, sacrificing their sons and daughters to devils, shedding innocent blood, *"even the blood of their sons and of their daughters, who they sacrificed unto the idols of Canaan: and the land was polluted with blood. Thus, were they defiled with their own works, and went a whoring with their own inventions."*

Celebrities and politicians endorse this evil in the name of "women's reproductive rights," but the truth is-- there is no difference between an abortion and sacrificing your son or daughter in the fire. The same ancient spirit that induced child sacrifice and idol worship then, is the same spirit working today. Most of these "pro-choice" groups are not prochoice but pro death promoting a culture of death. They *condemn the innocent and acquit the guilty* (Proverbs 17:15). Our state governments and judicial system have violated the *right to life* clause in the Constitution for the most vulnerable in our society: infants. To paraphrase, w*e have shed the blood of our sons and daughters and sacrificed them unto the idols: and the land (killing fields) was polluted with blood. Thus, we were defiled by our own works and prostituted ourselves with our own inventions (practices).*

Blood Covenants with Lucifer

Many world leaders, media moguls and entertainers have made blood covenants with Lucifer for power, fame, and wealth; Lucifer requires blood, and preferably, the blood of children as a sacrifice. In fact, many satanic rituals involve the rape, torture and killing of children. What are the consequences of making blood covenants with the fallen angel, Lucifer? In Genesis 4:10-11, the LORD said to Cain, *"What have you done? Listen! Your brother's blood cries out to me from the ground! And now art thou cursed from the earth, which hath opened her mouth to receive thy brother's blood crieth unto me from the ground."* The shedding of innocent blood brings about a curse on the land and people. In Genesis 9:6, God pronounces a curse on the one who sheds man's blood: *"Whoso sheddeth man's blood, by man shall his blood be shed: for in the image of God made he man."* In Leviticus 17:14, God warns his people to abstain from eating blood, *"Ye shall eat the blood of no manner of flesh; for the life of all flesh is the blood thereof; whosoever eateth it shall be cut off."* Satanic covenants or pacts require the eating of flesh (cannibalism) and the drinking of human blood. Many elites and celebrities who want to be successful in their careers must pledge their allegiance to Lucifer by making blood covenants.

According to Mosaic law, all things are cleansed with blood and without the shedding of blood, there can be no forgiveness (Hebrews 9:22). If you have made a blood covenant with Lucifer, the Scriptures says, *"In Him we have redemption through his blood, the forgiveness of sins, in accordance with the riches of God's grace"* (Ephesians 1:7). Only the blood of Jesus can break demonic pacts, curses.

Covetousness and Idol Worship

In Exodus 20:3-5, God said, *"Thou shalt have no other gods before me."* This meant that the people were not to worship or serve other gods other than the one true God, yet despite this warning, they disobeyed, bowing down to Canaanite deities. Today, the gods of this age are not necessarily carved of wood and stone but born of the flesh (evil nature) such as the love of money and pleasure. This world system has banished God's commandments from its institutions and forums and replaced it with doctrines of devils: *"Now the Spirit speaketh expressly, that in the latter times some shall depart from the faith, giving heed to seducing spirits, and doctrines of devils"* (1 Timothy 4:1). As technology becomes increasingly accessible, we are tempted and drawn away by it. We heed its voice and message rather than God's: *"I tell you the truth, whoever hears my word and believes him who sent me has eternal life and will not be condemned"* (John 5:24). On social media, we covet what we see, so *"each one is tempted when he is carried away and enticed by his own lust"* (James 1:14). We covet or lust after what we see to satisfy our selfish desires, *"So the eyes of man are never satisfied"* (Proverbs 27:20). In Exodus 20:17, the LORD declares, *"You shall not covet your neighbor's house; you shall not covet your neighbor's wife, or his male servant or his female servant or anything that belongs to your neighbor.*" But who is our neighbor? Today, our neighbor is anyone on social media and web forums. We are seduced and enslaved by temporary pleasures and things. Corporate giants and the elites are our puppet masters.

In our rebellion, we have become slaves of sin: *"Don't you know that when you offer yourselves to someone as obedient slaves, you are slaves of the one you obey—whether you are slaves to sin, which leads to death, or to obedience , which leads to righteousness?"* (Romans 6:16). Who do you obey? Do you obey your selfish desires and ambitions? If so, you must renounce sin and die to yourself. You must tune out the voices of this world and separate yourself from the unclean thing.

Everything we are shown on social media, the internet or TV is meant to distract, entice, and entrap us. This world system is like the sirens of Greek mythology who lured nearby sailors with their enchanting music and singing voices to shipwreck. Therefore, we are drawn away by what we see, and in the pursuit of it, we become a slave to it, for *"No one can serve two masters. Either you will hate one and love the other, or you will be devoted to the one and despise the other"* Matthew 6:24. Hence, we must choose life or death, God or the world system, for *"if any man loves the world, the love of the Father is not in* him," (1 John 2:15-17). Therefore, the LORD urges us to separate ourselves from the world, *"Wherefore come out from among them, and be ye separate, saith the Lord, and touch not the unclean thing; and I will receive you"* (2 Corinthians 6:17).

A certain ruler approached Jesus and asked him, *"'What shall I do to inherit eternal life?' And Jesus responded, 'Do not commit adultery, Do not kill, Do not steal, Do not bear false witness, Honor thy father and thy mother.' And he said, 'All these have I kept from youth up.' Now when Jesus heard these things, he said unto him, 'Yet lackest thou one thing: sell all that thou hast, and distribute unto the poor, and thou shalt have treasure in heaven: and come, follow me.' And when he heard this, he was very sorrowful: for he was very rich."* And what is the lesson here? If you want to keep your soul, you must first follow the commandments of God, give up all your idols (fleshly desires) and pursue Jesus. You must strip off the old man (nature) and put on the new man *"And be renewed in the spirit of your mind"* (Ephesians 4:23). We are not to let sin rule in our mortal bodies, nor obey the lusts thereof. Neither surrender to our members as instruments of unrighteousness unto sin: but submit unto God as instruments of righteousness unto God. For sin shall not have dominion over us (Romans 6:12-14).

Seducing Spirits of the World

Social media, animation, movies, videos, games, and books promote witchcraft, divination, sorcery, and other abominable practices. These are the *seducing spirits of the world*. In 1 Timothy 4:1, Timothy points to a sign of the end times, *"Now the Spirit speaketh expressly, that in the latter times some shall depart from the faith, giving heed to seducing (lying) spirits, and doctrines (teachings) of devils"* (1 Timothy 4:1). These are sent out throughout the whole world via social media, TV and other electronic means, seducing and enticing young people to dabble in the occult. The enemy has used technology for decades to entice young people into the dark arts. He will use games, books, videos, movies, and shows to distract and trap our souls. We must guard our hearts (soul), eye and ear gates from such influence.

The devil knows our weaknesses and fears and will use them to destroy us. For example, after Saul was rejected by God, Saul desperately sought the counsel of Samuel, the prophet. Despite banning all mediums and those who consult the spirits of the dead from Israel, Saul broke his own laws to consult a medium and summon the spirit of Samuel for direction (1 Samuel 31:1-6); Saul *imitated* the detestable practices of the pagans to seek direction and met a tragic end. In Acts 19:18-20, we see that

[120]

many new believers confessed to the sin of sorcery and witchcraft:

> *"Many of those who believed now came and*
> *openly confessed their evil deeds. A number who*
> *had practiced sorcery brought their scrolls*
> *together and burned them publicly. When they*
> *calculated the value of the scrolls, the total came*
> *to fifty thousand drachmas. In this way the word*
> *of the Lord spread widely and grew in power."*

Notice that once they renounced the occult, *the word of the Lord spread* and *grew in power.* In this verse, the word *power* in the Greek means *force or strength to overcome.* You cannot overcome the enemy from your own strength, but from the Holy Spirit. Many young people dabble in the occult to gain power, but real power comes from God alone; the enemy will deceive and manipulate you with supernatural giftings such as psychic abilities, but such are just *imitations* of God's real power and gifts.

Warnings about Mediums, Necromancers and Diviners

The Bible warns us about turning to mediums, necromancers, and astrologers. A medium or necromancer is one who speaks to the dead or *familiar spirits* (generational demons) to use or enter his or her body for the purpose of foretelling events. An astrologer or diviner is one who practices foretelling the future by reading signs and omens. These practices are directly opposed to God because they violate His law: *"Do not turn to mediums or necromancers; do not seek them out, and so make yourselves unclean by them: I am the LORD your God"* (Leviticus 19:31).

We see the anger of the Lord kindled against those who violate His law. Today, we see leaders and politicians use divination, sorcery, and magic to influence and gain power. Divination and idol worship are practiced in prominent levels of our government and the entertainment industry. Surprisingly, the use of Egyptian symbology, child sacrifice and pagan rituals are commonly practiced in the high echelons of society among the elites and powerful. Yet, there is a prophecy concerning them: *And the spirit of Egypt shall fail in the midst thereof; and I will destroy the counsel thereof: and they shall seek to the idols, and to the charmers, and to them that have familiar spirits, and to the wizards* (Isaiah 19:3). The LORD will expose those who practice such things, and all their sorcery and curses will fail, yet they will not repent of their wicked ways. Such was the case with Manassah, in 2 Kings 21:6: *"And he made his son pass through the fire, practiced witchcraft, and used divination, and dealt with mediums and spiritists. He did much evil in the sight of the Lord provoking Him to anger."*

God forbids divination or astrology because only God knows the future. We see this in the Old Testament when God sends prophets to speak to the nation of Israel to warn them. God said, *"I make known the end from the beginning, from ancient times, what is still to come. I say: 'My purpose will stand, and I will do all that I please"* (Isaiah 46:10). God makes known his power and will to Israel in the confrontation between the false prophets of Baal and Elijah on Mount Carmel (1 Kings 18:20-40). He openly defies the false prophets (diviners, astrologers, wizards) and argues with them who do not know the future:

Produce your cause, saith the LORD; bring forth your strong reasons, saith the King of Jacob. Let them bring them forth, and shew us what shall happen: let them shew the former things, what they be, that we may consider them, and know the latter end of them; or declare us things for to come, Shew the things that are to come hereafter, that we may know that ye are gods: yea, do good, or do evil, that we may be dismayed, and behold it together. Behold, ye are of nothing, and your work of nought: an abomination is he that chooseth you. Who hath declared from the beginning, that we may know? And before time, that we may say, He is righteous? Yea, there is none that sheweth, yea, there is none that declareth, yea, there is none that heareth your words" (Isaiah 41:21 KJV).

[123]

God also has the power of life and death. For example, Matthew writes, *"Do not be afraid of those who kill the body but cannot kill the soul. Rather, be afraid of the One who can destroy both soul and body in hell"* (Matthew 10:28). Father God determines our eternal destiny after we die; therefore, we should fear Him. In our arrogance and foolishness, we assume control of our life and destiny, but the truth is that we cannot even control our own death or what happens tomorrow:

> *"Come now, you who say, 'Today or tomorrow we will go to such and such a city, spend a year there, buy and sell, and make a profit'; whereas you do not know what will happen tomorrow. For what is your life? It is even a vapor that appears for a little time and then vanishes away"* (James 4:13-14).

Furthermore, God has the power to extend your life or cut it short. For example, God heard King Hezekiah's prayer on his sick bed, saw his tears and granted him an extension of life: *"I have heard your prayer; I have seen your tears. Look, I will add fifteen years to your life"* (Isaiah 38:5). God has the power not only to add life but to also cut it short: *"The fear of the LORD adds length to life, but the years of the wicked are cut short"* (Proverbs 10:27).

Jesus' ministry on earth also manifested God's formidable power over devils, sickness and even death. After Jesus' death, the Bible details that he spent three days and three nights in the heart of the earth and triumphed over death and Hades (hell). Jesus returned to life with resurrection power to declare victory over the enemy. In short, the enemy was defeated at the cross. When Jesus died on the cross, God's Word was fulfilled in Genesis, *"And I will put enmity between you and the woman, and between your offspring and hers; he will crush your head and you will strike his heel"* (Genesis 3:15). Satan's head was crushed. The *head* represents authority, so Satan was stripped of his authority and power over us.

Hence, when we dabble in the occult, we are giving the devil a foothold (our heel), but the Bible says, *"and do not give the devil a foothold"* (Ephesians 4:27). In other words, we should not open the door to demonic influences, doctrines, or practices because they will deceive, manipulate, torment, and ultimately destroy you.

Games

According to a new study from the family technology education non-profit group Common Sense Media, teens spend an average of nine hours a day of screen time while preteens spend 6 hours per day on their phones. [1] Most preteens play games and watch videos on their phones, while older kids do much of the same. It is no wonder that this last generation has been exposed to more pornography, sexual perversion, violence, vanity, cruelty than ever before. The knowledge of good and evil is increasing increasingly, and children as young as two are being indoctrinated by the *seducing spirits of this world*. One-way seducing spirits are trapping children and teens are games. Online free games are the number one form of entertainment for children and teens. Children will easily ignore family, friends, church, duties, and responsibilities to play games or watch videos, so what is the solution? Paul writes *"So be on your guard, not asleep like the others. Stay alert and be clearheaded"* (1 Thessalonians 5:6). If you are playing games, you are asleep to the real purpose of your life. You were not created to spend hours of your precious life playing games. Jesus did not die on the cross, so that you can entertain and indulge yourself. In fact, In John 10:10, Jesus says, *"The thief cometh not, but for to steal, and to kill, and to destroy I am come that they might have life and that they might have it more abundantly."* The thief represents *seducing spirits* (demons) that come to steal your time, health, money, gifts, abilities, and God-given purpose. The thief comes when the owner of the house is asleep or not vigilant. This generation has been bombarded by the enemy with all kinds of distractions resulting in an increase of sin and unrighteousness. In 2 Timothy 3: 1-5, Timothy writes the vision of the last generation:

> *"There will be terrible times in the last days. People will be lovers of themselves, lovers of money, boastful, proud, abusive, disobedient to their parents, ungrateful, unholy, without love, unforgiving, slanderous, without self-control, brutal, not lovers of the good, treacherous, rash, conceited, lovers of pleasure rather than lovers of God—having a form of godliness but denying its power. Have nothing to do with such people."*

This generation has become *lovers of pleasure rather than lovers of God*. We have forsaken the commandments of God to worship the gods of pleasure and self. The Bible says that we will all appear before the *judgment seat of Christ or the final judgment to account for what we did while on earth whether for good or evil* (2 Corinthians 5:10). Therefore, do not be foolish, but make the most of your time. King David wrote, "*So teach us to number our days, that we may apply our hearts to wisdom*" (Psalm 90:12).

Many young people use games to mask depression, boredom, anxiety, or fear, but Jesus says, *"Peace I leave with you, my peace I give unto you: not as the world giveth, give I unto you. Let not your heart be troubled, neither let it be afraid"* (John 14:27) Jesus wants to give you peace of mind, not as the *world gives* through distractions or *supernormal stimuli* such as games, junk food, pornography, or the internet. The peace of God *"surpasses all understanding"* and *"will guard your hearts and your minds in Christ Jesus"* (Philippians 4:7)

How can the devil take away your peace and destroy your soul with games? The game will contain subtle but disturbing messages and images that will defile your spirit. Games will function as a portal attracting seducing (lying) spirits, searing your conscience, and polluting your thoughts and imagination. Games can create strongholds of violence, fear, depression and even attract spirits of death and suicide. Parents should monitor their child's internet activity and game time to prevent exposure.

The devil, our adversary, has been around from the beginning of time and knows how to push our buttons. We must put on the weapons of warfare and fight the good fight; otherwise, he will destroy us. You MUST put away the games and distractions and seek the LORD and His kingdom if you want to live an abundant life: *"I have come that they may have life, and that they may have it more abundantly"* (John 10:9-10). What is the abundant life? When you invite the Holy Spirit to come and live inside of you, your spirit man is *born again,* and Jesus fills your *golden cup* (spirit man) with *living water* or life from above. In other words, you become a new creation in Christ. Jesus said, *"Very truly I tell you, no one can see the kingdom of God unless they are born again"* (John 3:3). The enemy doesn't ever want you to experience this rebirth of the spirit, enjoy the benefits of an abundant life or fulfill your destiny in Christ, so he has devised a plan to steal, kill and destroy you; understand that the devil does not come at you directly with horns and a pitchfork, he will use *temptation* to lure you away from God. When Jesus retreated to the wilderness for 40 days and 40 nights to fast and pray, the devil tempted him with carnal pleasures and desires, but each time he was tempted, Jesus resisted the devil by quoting scripture and denying himself. To defeat the devil, we must quote scripture and deny ourselves or resist our carnal desires for self-indulgence and pleasure-seeking.

[1] "Teens spend nearly nine hours every day consuming media," The Washington Post: http://www.washingtonpost.com/news/the-switch/wp/2015/11/03/teens-spend-nearly-nine-hours-every-day-consuming-media/.

The Lotus-Eaters

In Greek mythology, the lotus-eaters were a race of people living on an island overrun by lotus plants. Lotus fruits and flowers were the primary food on the island and were a narcotic or strong drug causing the inhabitants to sleep in blissful apathy. In the epic tale of the Odyssey Book IX, Odysseus, a Greek hero sailing home to Ithaca after the Trojan War, is blown off course by heavy north winds to the land of the lotus-eaters. After landing, the crew met the inhabitants of the island who offered them the lotus, and they did eat of it, forgetting all their troubles and cared not about returning home. The lotus drug made them lazy and forgetful, so that they forgot their mission or purpose. Interestingly, a "lotus-eater" denotes "a person who spends time indulging in pleasure and luxury rather than dealing with practical concerns."

God detests laziness and self-indulgence. In Proverbs 6:9-11, it says, *"How long will you lie down, O sluggard? When will you arise from your sleep? A little sleep, a little slumber, A little folding of the hands to rest—Your poverty will come in like a vagabond and your need like an armed man."* Understand that games and distractions make you forget your real purpose—to serve the God of creation. The devil knows how to make you forget or escape; he lures you with entertainment and pleasure, but sadly, the high only lasts for a moment and then it's gone. The Apostle John writes, *"For everything in the world—the lust of the flesh, the lust of the eyes, and the pride of life—comes not from the Father but from the world"* (1 John 2:16). The *spirit of this world* is tempting you just as he tempted Jesus in the wilderness, but you must deny yourself (carnal self) and resist, just like our Greek hero—Odysseus. You see, after he realized the lotus fruit caused most of his crew to slumber and forget, he immediately gathered up his men, returned to the ship and left the island. Likewise, you must awake, repent, or turn around and follow Christ.

Doctrines of Devils

The enemy means to deceive you with *Doctrines of demons* or (false teachings) about reincarnation and the afterlife: *"The Spirit clearly says that in later times some will abandon the faith and follow deceiving spirits and things taught by demons"* (1 Timothy 4:1). We see this deception spread by popular culture today through movies, songs and even holidays, but according to Hebrews 9:27, *"It is appointed unto men once to die, but after this the judgment."* Reincarnation is not to be confused with the first and second resurrection of the dead. Its roots are found in the Eastern religions such as Hinduism, Buddhism, Sikhism and Jainism, and it is the philosophical and religious concept that a soul must undergo a cyclic existence of deaths and rebirths. This, of course, is a perversion of the truth. In 2 Corinthians 5:8, Paul writes, *"We are confident, I say, and willing rather to be absent from the body, and to be present with the Lord."* In other words, after your body dies, your soul will be present with the Lord to face judgment. We will appear before God's throne to give an account of our life whether good or bad (2 Corinthians 5:10).

The Spirit of Death

In Mexico, the spirit of death has its own holiday, Day of the Dead (Día de los Muertos) dating back three thousand years ago with the Aztecs; the Aztecs believed that after death, the soul traveled to Chicunamictian, the Land of the Dead. The soul then had to journey through nine levels of hell to reach Mictian, the final resting place. Traditionally, family members leave food, water, tools, and other offerings on graves to help the deceased in their journey. In medieval Spain, family members would leave wine and bread on the graves of their loved ones. In Europe, pagan celebrations of the dead consisted of bonfires, dancing, and feasting. European settlers later introduced this pagan tradition to the North American continent. For example, in the United States, *Halloween* or *All Saints Day*, renamed by the

Catholic church, is celebrated in October during the Jewish holiday of Yom Kippur.

The Ancient origins of Halloween date back to the pagan Celtic festival of Samhain. The Celts believed that the dead walked among the living. During Samhain, the living could visit with the dead. According to the book *Halloween—An American Holiday, An American History*, Celts disguised themselves in costumes made of animal skins to confuse the wandering spirits, lit bonfires and offered human and animal sacrifices to appease the spirits.

Today, our culture celebrates the spirit of death year 'round through abortions, suicides, occult practices, drug abuse, violence, euthanasia, genocide, war, and terrorism. We do not need a special holiday to honor death; it's all around us. Our culture has become so desensitized to *death* through the media and entertainment industry, that we have become *"comfortably numb"* to it. What must we do to keep ourselves pure from this spirit? We should turn away from it. King David writes, *"I will refuse to look at anything vile and vulgar. I hate all who deal crookedly; I will have nothing to do with them."* (Psalm 101:3). So how do we protect ourselves from the spirit of death? We must first repent and confess our sins to God, for He is merciful to forgive; secondly, we must renounce the spirit of death and call upon the name of Jesus Christ. We must ask for the Holy Spirit, *"If ye then being evil know how to give good gifts unto your children; how much more shall your heavenly Father give the Holy Spirit to them that ask him?* "(Luke 11:13). Then, we must declare with our lips, *"I will not die, but live, And declare the works of the LORD"* (Psalm 118:17) and boldly proclaim, *"For you will not leave my soul among the dead or allow your holy one to rot in the grave"* (Psalm 16:10). Finally, we must choose life, and speak words of life over ourselves and others.

Spirit of Fashion

Satan uses subtle and not so subtle ways to trap your soul. For example, young people may give direct legal entry to demonic oppression, death, and spiritual bondage through associations such as (gangs, religious rites, drugs, the occult) and not so subtle ways through (tattoos, music, cosmetics, jewelry, popular hair and clothing styles, etc....). The Book of Enoch references the fallen angel, Azazel, who taught the women to make bracelets, ornaments, rings and necklaces from precious metals and stones. He also showed them how to beautify their eyelids with kohl and cosmetic tricks to attract and seduce the opposite sex. From these practices Enoch says there came much 'godlessness' and men and women committed fornication, were led astray and became corrupt in their ways.

Therefore, what you wear may attract demons and open ancient doors. Occult jewelry with tribal, gothic, satanic symbols, skulls, inverted pentagrams, and talismans invite demonic oppression and possession. Demons attach themselves to these objects, so they must be discarded and eliminated. Even necklaces and wrist bands that resemble chains or snakes are designed from the pit of hell. Many fashion trends and products are cursed, inspired by demons, and brought to the world. For example, many name brand cosmetics and perfumes use aborted fetal tissue. The Word declares:

> "Adulterers and adulteresses! Do you not know that friendship with the world is enmity with God? Whoever therefore wants to be a friend of the world makes himself an enemy of God" James 4:4 and "The world and its desires pass away, but whoever does the will of God lives forever" 1 John 2:17.

Goth, punk, emo fashions have been made popular by worldly musicians, artists, and entertainers. Fashion trends usually emerge from subcultures of a society until they become normalized and mainstreamed; For example, cosmetic and fashion trends now celebrate and normalize the LGTBQ+ subculture. Another trend celebrated and popularized are sagging pants that may have started with gangs or the gay subculture in the prison system.

In addition, tattoos once considered taboo in western civilizations, are now mainstream and wildly popular. Tattoos date back to the third century BC. Cultures from around the world have practiced tattooing and piercing such as the pagan nations that surrounded Israel. The LORD warned Israel to not imitate the customs and practices of the gentiles, *"Do not cut your bodies for the dead or put tattoo marks on yourselves. I am the LORD"* Leviticus 19:28. In short, the LORD warns us to *"Be alert and of sober mind. Your enemy the devil prowls around like a roaring lion looking for someone to devour"* In 1 Peter 5:8.

Therefore, do not be seduced by the world's fashion, cosmetic trends, and styles; these are traps of the enemy that can lead you astray. Therefore, the Scriptures say, *"Don't copy the behavior and customs of this world, but let God transform you into a new person by changing the way you think. Then you will learn to know God's will for you, which is good, pleasing, and perfect"* (Romans 12:2). I pray that your eyes of your understanding may be opened to the devices of the enemy.

The Three Wise Monkeys

The ancient Japanese symbol of *the three wise monkeys* holds a particularly important message for us today: *Mizaru*, covering his eyes, sees no evil, *Kikazaru*, covering his ears, hears no evil and *Iwazaru*, covering his mouth speaks no evil. If you want to keep your soul and remain pure, you must close the gates. There are four main gaits to the soul: the eye, ear, mind, and heart gates. The spirit of death, perversion, violence, and all unrighteousness enter through the gates, so let's consider each one.

Temptation enters through the eye gate. Jesus said, *"And if your eye causes you to stumble, gouge it out and throw it away. It is better for you to enter life with one eye than to have two eyes and be thrown into the fire of hell."* (Matthew 19:9). So, our eyes can cause us to sin when we *covet or lust*. To covet or lust, means to desire wrongfully, so sin enters when we covet *with our eyes* after the *things* of this world. In the Garden of Eden, the fruit itself was not evil, but *covetousness* led to Adam and Eve's downfall. You see, God told them to eat of every fruit of the trees of the garden except for the fruit of the *tree of knowledge of good and evil*, but they disobeyed and lusted after forbidden fruit. In James 4:2, lust brings forth death and destruction: *"Ye lust, and have not, ye kill, and desire to have, and cannot obtain: ye fight and war, yet ye have not, because ye ask not.*" For example, we see the effects of lust on King David's life when he lusted after Bathsheba. In 2 Samuel 11-12, we read that King David got up from his bed, walked around the roof and saw a woman bathing and the woman was exceptionally beautiful, so David sent someone to find out about her. He learned that the woman was the wife of Uriah the Hittite. Despite this fact, he slept with her, and she became pregnant. To conceal the pregnancy, he ordered the death of Uriah. As a result, the spirit of death entered the House of David. God spoke and said, *"Now therefore the sword shall never depart from thine house; because thou hast despised me, and hast taken the wife of Uriah the Hittite to be thy wife."* Like Adam and Eve, King David could have had the fruit of any tree of the garden, but he chose the forbidden fruit.

In short, we are to be content with what God has given us, and not covet the *things* of the world, but unfortunately, our eyes are never satisfied, *"Hell and destruction are never full; so, the eyes of man are never satisfied"* (Proverbs 27:20). Paul warns us, *"Nor thieves, nor the greedy, nor drunkards, nor revilers, nor swindlers will inherit the kingdom of God"* (1 Corinthians 6:10). Thus, our insatiable greed or pursuit of material possessions (obsession with *things*) brings eternal consequences.

The second monkey covers his ears or hears no evil. How is it possible to hear no evil? Romans 10:17 says, *"Faith cometh by hearing, and hearing by the word of God."* The Word of God renews, sanctifies, and gives us life. In Deuteronomy 8:3, we read: *"Man shall not live by bread alone; but by every word that proceeds from the mouth of the LORD."* We must shut out all the other voices, philosophies, or doctrines of devils, and we must listen to the Holy Spirit: *"My sheep hear my voice, and I know them, and they follow me"* (John 10:27). You must be able to recognize the voice of the shepherd and the hired hand. The voice of the shepherd will always align itself with the Word of God, but the enemy will pervert the Word to lead you astray, so how do we discern the truth? The Holy Spirit imparts revelation or wisdom when we read the Word of God, so you must first be born again. Once you receive the Holy Spirit, *"he will guide you into all truth. He will not speak on his own; he will speak only what he hears, and he will tell you what is yet to come"* (John 16:13).

How do we shut out the voices of the world? We must pursue righteousness and holiness, *"for it is written: 'Be holy, because I am holy"* (1 Peter 1:16). Holiness comes when we read and wash our eyes with the Word: *"to make her holy, cleansing her by the washing with water through the Word"* (Ephesians

5:26). What does this mean? It means we need to stop listening to music, shows, videos or games that grieve the Holy Spirit: *"And grieve not the holy Spirit of God, whereby ye are sealed unto the day of redemption"* (Ephesians 4:30 KJV). We must seek after the Kingdom of God, and *"run from anything that stimulates youthful lusts. Instead, pursue righteous living, faithfulness, love, and peace* (2 Timothy 2:22).

The third monkey covers his mouth or speaks no evil. What does this mean? It means that evil comes from within. Speaking to a group of pharisees and knowing what was in their hearts, Jesus said, *"O generation of vipers, how can ye, being evil, speak good things? For out of the abundance of the heart the mouth speaketh"* (Matthew 12:34). The heart (soul) is our conscience, will and emotions. The Apostle Paul writes, *"the work of the law written in their hearts, their conscience also bearing witness, and between themselves [their] thoughts accusing or else excusing [them]"* (Romans 2:15 NKJV). In other words, our conscience bears witness to the truth, so we can either justify our sin, or repent. Because we have eaten the fruit of the *tree of knowledge of good and evil*, God has *written in our hearts* an understanding of right and wrong. You do not have to be born again to know the difference between what is good or evil. For example, in John 8:1-11, the pharisees brought a woman to be stoned for adultery to Jesus saying, *"Now Moses, in the law, commanded us that such should be stoned. What do You say?"* but Jesus knowing their *hearts* stooped down and wrote on the stony ground with His finger (a new law), and when pressed again, He stood up and said to them: *"He who is without sin among you, let him throw the first stone."* Those who heard it, *"being convicted by their conscience, went out one by one."* Jesus knew their hearts or secret sins. Therefore, to speak no evil, we must open our hearts to Jesus. In Revelation 3:20, Jesus said, *"Here I am! I stand at the door and knock. If anyone hears my voice and opens the door, I will come in and eat with that person, and they with me."* The *door* represents the heart (soul). We must open the *door of our heart* and invite the Holy Spirit to come in and eat with us (communion).

The Spirit of Sorcery [Pharmakoi]

If you are addicted to drugs and/or alcohol, God wants to deliver and heal you. Drugs and alcohol are snares or weapons of the enemy, but the blood of Christ has the power to destroy and defeat the enemy. In Revelations 18, John describes mystery Babylon as *"the dwelling place of demons, a prison for every foul spirit, and a cage for every unclean and hated bird."* He foretells her destruction and those *"who became rich by her, will stand at a distance for fear of her torment, weeping and wailing."* These merchants (dealers) were the *great men of the earth* who *"for by your sorcery all the nations were deceived."* The term sorcery or [pharmakoi] refers to magic or magic arts and includes drugs used for magical spells. Drugs, potions, or herbs were used in the occult to open portals. Those who come under the influence of the spirit of pharmakoi put themselves in a drug-induced state to open *chakras*, doorways, or portals, to demonic spirits. However, the LORD will judge the nations for their sorceries. For example, the LORD rebuked Israel for her rebellion and sorceries, *"Stand now with your enchantments and the multitude of your sorceries* (Isaiah 47:12). It is because of the multitude of her sorceries that her destruction has come, *"Both of these will overtake you in a moment, on a single day: loss of children and widowhood. They will come upon you in full measure, despite your many sorceries and all your potent spells"* (Isaiah 47:9). Of Nineveh, the prophet Nahum described the city as *"the mistress of sorceries, who sells nations through her harlotries, and families through her sorceries"* and *"A great number of bodies, countless corpses—They stumble over the corpses—Because of the multitude of harlotries of the seductive harlot"* (Nahum 3:3-5). Hence, the spirit of pharmakoi is a deceiving spirit from the pit of hell sent to seduce and destroy the nations.

The Bible describes how in the last days, the wicked would *"not repent of their murders or their sorceries or their sexual immorality or their thefts"* (Revelations 9:21). In 1 Peter 5:8-9, Peter warns the young, *"Be alert and of sober mind. Your enemy the devil prowls around like a roaring lion looking for someone to devour."* The word *sober* means to abstain from *spirits*. Thus, a person under the influence of pharmakoi can be demonically possessed and die. In Revelation 21:8, those who practice sorcery *"shall have their part in the lake which burns with fire and brimstone, which is the second death."* If you are under this spirit's influence, you must renounce it and confess Jesus as your Lord and Savior.

Pray this prayer out loud:

Jesus, have mercy on me, a sinner. With a contrite and broken heart, I ask for forgiveness and healing, for you say in your Word that "You will not reject a broken and repentant heart, O God" (Psalm 51:17). I will bless the LORD, O my soul, and forget not all His benefits: Who forgives me of all my iniquities, who heals me of all my diseases, who redeems my life from destruction and crowns me with lovingkindness and tender mercies, who satisfies my mouth with good things, so that my youth is renewed like the eagle's (Psalm 103:3-5). Today, I renounce - (name all the drugs), the spirit of pharmakoi, and make a covenant with you this day - (date) to serve you. I confess you as my Lord and Savior. I believe you died on the cross for me; therefore, I submit my body, soul, and spirit to you. Restore to me all the parts of my soul and lead me in the paths of righteousness for your name's sake (Psalm 23:3). The Lord of Hosts delivers me from my strong enemy, from those who hate me, for they are too strong for me (Psalm 18:17). With a strong hand, and with an outstretched arm, your mercy [endures] forever (Psalm 136:12). For who is powerful enough to enter the house of a strong man and plunder his goods? Only someone even stronger—someone who could tie him up and then plunder his house (Matthew 12:29).

Lord, bind up the strongman and plunder his house. Return to me my possessions. If my mind and body have been damaged by evil, restore, and renew it. Search me O God and know my heart. Try me and know my thoughts: And see if there is any wicked way in me and lead me in the way everlasting (Psalm 139: 23-24). Cover me with your precious blood and make me invisible to the enemy. "Guard my life and rescue me; do not let me be put to shame, for I take refuge in you" (Psalm 25:20). I put my trust in you, Lord. "My hope is in You" (Psalm 39:7).

Prayer of Deliverance

Lord do not punish me in your anger or discipline me in your wrath. For your arrows have sunk into me, and your hand has pressed down on me. There is no soundness in my body because of your indignation; there is no health in my bones because of my sin. For my iniquities have flooded over my head; they are a burden too heavy for me to bear. My wounds are foul and festering because of my foolishness. I am bent over and brought incredibly low; all day long I go around mourning. For my insides are full of burning pain and there is no soundness in my body. I am faint and severely crushed; I groan because of the anguish of my heart. Lord, my every desire is in front of you; my sighing is not hidden from you. My heart races, my strength leaves me, and even the light of my eyes has faded. My loved ones and friends stand back from my affliction, and my relatives stand at a distance.

Those who intend to kill me set traps, and those who want to harm me threaten to destroy me; they plot treachery all day long. I am like a deaf person; I do not hear. I am like a speechless person who does not open his mouth. I am like a man who does not hear and has no arguments in his mouth. For I put my hope in you, LORD: you will answer me, my Lord, my God. For I said, "Don't let them rejoice over me—those who are arrogant toward me when I stumble." For I am about to fall, and my pain is constantly with me. So, I confess my iniquity; I am anxious because of my sin. But my enemies are vigorous and powerful; many hate me for no reason. Those who repay evil for good attack me for pursuing good. Lord do not abandon me; my God, do not be far from me. Hurry to help me, my Lord, my salvation (Psalm 38).

The sorrows of death compassed me, and the floods of ungodly men made me afraid. The sorrows of hell compassed me about: the snares of death prevented me. In my distress I called upon the LORD and cried unto my God: he heard my voice out of his temple, and my cry came before him, even into his ears (Psalm 18:4-6). He delivered me from my strong enemy, and from them which hated me: for they were too strong for me (Psalm 18:17).

Thank the LORD for your healing, deliverance and praise Him with song and dance. Play worship music and meditate on the WORD.

CHAPTER SIX

The Sin of Rebellion

"For rebellion is as the sin of witchcraft, and stubbornness is as iniquity and idolatry." –Samuel 15:23 KJV

The LORD hates rebellion: to illustrate this, I will take you to Numbers 16, and the story of *Korah's rebellion*. Korah along with two hundred and fifty prominent Israelite leaders of the community and representatives of the assembly rebelled against Moses. According to the account, these young men complained that Moses had appointed himself priest and ruler over the congregation, and claimed that they had the same priestly authority as Aaron and his sons; at hearing this, Moses fell facedown and then instructed Korah and his followers to take firepans, place fire in them and put incense on them before the LORD, and let the LORD choose who will be a priest, so each man took his firepan, placed fire in it, put incense on it, and stood at the entrance to the tent of meeting along with Moses and Aaron. After Korah assembled the whole congregation against them at the entrance to the tent of meeting, the glory of the LORD appeared to them. Then, the LORD spoke to Moses and Aaron, *"Separate yourselves from them, so I may consume them instantly."* But Moses and Aaron fell facedown and pleaded with God to spare the community, so the LORD replied to Moses, *"Tell the community: Get away from the dwellings of Korah, Dathan, and Abiram."* Moses warned the community to separate themselves or be swept away in judgment for their sins, so Moses told the congregation, *"If these men die naturally as all people would, and suffer the fate of all, then the LORD has not sent me. But if the LORD brings about something unprecedented, and the ground opens its mouth and swallows them along with all that belongs to them so that they go down alive into Sheol, then you will know that these men have displeased the LORD."* And just as he finished speaking all these words, the ground beneath them opened. The earth opened its mouth and swallowed them and their households—Korah's people and their possessions. They went down alive into Sheol (hell) with all that belonged to them. The earth closed over them, and they vanished from the assembly. So, what is the moral of this story? God has appointed rulers over you, and it is not your place to murmur or complain but submit to them.

What is rebellion, how does it manifest and what is the penalty? In 1 Samuel 15:23, rebellion is compared to the sin of divination (witchcraft): *"For rebellion is like the sin of divination, and defiance is like wickedness and idolatry. Because you have rejected the word of the LORD, he has rejected you as king.* In this account, Samuel the prophet instructed King Saul to go and attack the *Amalekites* and destroy everything they had: *"Do not spare them. Kill men and women, infants and nursing babies, oxen and sheep, camels, and donkeys."*

The Amalekites were a ruthless and bloody people, enemies of the Israelites, so the LORD wanted to eradicate them; however, Saul disobeyed and instead followed his heart and eyes. Saul spared King Agag, and the best of the sheep, goats, cattle, and choice animals, as well as the young rams and the best of everything else. As a result, Samuel admonished Saul: *"Look to obey is better than sacrifice, to pay attention is better than the fat of rams...because you have rejected the word of the LORD, he has rejected you as king."* King Saul rebelled or turned away from the LORD's commands to follow his own heart and eyes, and as a result, the LORD turned away from Saul and rejected him as King.

Rebellion is disobedience to authority and following your own way. The most famous story of rebellion was the fall of Lucifer, the archangel. In Isaiah 14:12-15, the LORD describes the fall:

"How you are fallen from heaven, O Lucifer, son of the morning! How you are cut down to the ground, you who weakened the nations! For you have said in your heart: I will ascend into heaven, I will exalt my throne above the stars of God; I will also sit on the mount of the congregation On the farthest sides of the north; I will ascend above the heights of the clouds, I will be like the Most High. Yet you shall be brought down to Sheol, To the lowest depths of the Pit."

In short, Lucifer and his angels were cast out, brought down to the lowest depths of the pit, and from there, they entice and deceive the entire world to rebel against God. These are the origins of sin, but why did God permit this rebellion? For this, we must look at the law of will.

The Law of Will

God has given the law of will. It is the law of will that allows men and angels to choose: *"Choose this day whom you will serve"* (Joshua 24:15) and *"Today I have given you the choice between life and death, between blessings and curses"* (Deuteronomy 30:19). We are all presented with choices: *"Thousands upon thousands are waiting in the valley of decision.*

There the day of the LORD will soon arrive" (Joel 3:14). The choices we make in this life will determine our eternal destiny.

Thus, Satan understands the law of will. He knows the only way he can have access to your soul is if you grant him permission through sin or disobedience. If you sin willfully, God will turn you over to a *"reprobate mind."* A *reprobate mind* is the opposite of the *mind of Christ.* It is someone who has willfully rejected God's authority and leading. In 2 Timothy 3:8, Paul refers to those whose works are reprobate: *"They profess that they know God; but in works they deny him."*

Today, there are a lot of youths who claim to be Christian but deny Him through their actions and words. How can we deny Him through actions and words? Whenever, we *willfully* choose our own path without the direction, leading or covering of God, we deny Him. This opens the door for the enemy to reap havoc. The enemy will have the legal right to torment your soul and destroy your life. So how do we overcome? We must deny ourselves, assume our cross and follow him. We must let go and let God. In other words, we must surrender our will and agree with the will of God.

Jesus Christ understood the law of will. He submitted himself to the will of God even if that meant great suffering and death: *"Father, if you are willing, take this cup from me; yet not my will, but yours be done* (Luke 22:42). Jesus not only obeyed in actions, but in words: *"For I did not speak on my own, but the Father who sent me commanded me to say all that I have spoken"* (John 12:49). What does this mean for us today? It means that we are to submit to the will of God in all things. We are to die to our dreams, selfish ambitions, and pursuits: *"Do nothing out of selfish ambition or vain conceit. Rather, in humility value others above yourselves, not looking to your own interests but each of you to the interests of the others"* (Philippians 2:3-4). Hence, we were not born on this Earth to fulfill our own desires and plans. The Bible warns about making plans without God:

> *"Go to now, ye that say, Today or morrow we will go into such a city, and continue   there a year, and buy and sell, and get gain: whereas ye know not what shall be on the morrow. For what is your life? It is even a vapour, that appeareth for a little time, and then vanisheth away. For that ye ought to say, if the Lord will, we shall live, and do this, or that" (James 4:13-15).*

God created us with talents and gifts, not to glory in ourselves, but to glorify him. In fact, God will not share his glory with you.

[153]

He will use your shortcomings, not your strengths or talents to glorify himself. We see this in the life of Peter. God used a simple fisherman to preach to the devout Jews. The LORD declares, *"It is not by force nor by strength, but by my Spirit"* (Zechariah 4:6). We must surrender our choices and life to fulfill our God-given destiny, but to do this, we must be like sheep and obey his commandments. We must submit to authority and humble ourselves. Jesus set the example: *"For even the Son of Man did not come to be served, but to serve, and to give His life a ransom for many"* (Mark 10:45).

The Law of Authority

Another important law the enemy wants to you to ignore or violate is the law of authority: *"Honor your father and your mother, so that you may live long in the land the LORD your God is giving you."* —Exodus 20:12. Notice this is the only commandment with a promise. The promise is a long life, so if you violate the principle of authority—any authority—your life is cut short. God has appointed all authority: *"Let every soul be subject to the governing authorities. For there is no authority except from God, and the authorities that exist are appointed by God"* (Romans 13:1). Today, we see that young people are disrespectful to parents, teachers, police officers, employers, and other governing bodies.

The Lord makes it clear that those who rebel against authority will be severely judged. For example, Paul writes: *"Therefore whoever resists the authorities resists what God has appointed, and those who resist will incur judgment"* (Romans 13:1-5). In 2 Peter 2:10-15, Peter refers to those who subvert authority as *"cursed children," "presumptuous," "self-willed," "natural brute beasts"* who *walk in the flesh, speak evil of dignities, and despise government.* The *government* is the natural and supernatural order of God. In other words, there is a government on Earth and in Heaven. In the family, God ordained the husband to have authority over his wife: *"For the husband is the head of the wife as Christ is the head of the church, his body, of which he is Savior"* (Ephesians 5:23). Rebellion against God's authority was humanity's first sin in Genesis 3 and is a serious matter in God's eyes. God created a hierarchy in the family, church, and society. Without this hierarchy in place, there would be dysfunction and chaos. Paul continues, *"Therefore one must be in subjection, not only to avoid God's wrath but also for the sake of conscience."*

Some teens blame their parents for abuse, divorce etc.., however, despite parents' human weaknesses and flaws, God still expects children and teens to honor (respect) their parents and obey them. The enemy loves to stir up division and strife between parents and children. In fact, this is a widespread problem in our society. Today, children and teens are becoming increasingly rebellious thus fulfilling the end-time prophecy in 2 Timothy 3:3, *"They will be unloving and unforgiving: they will slander others and have no self-control. They will be cruel and hate what is good."* In short, please understand that Satan wants to take you down. He wants to trap you in sin and, kill you. That is the devil's master plan. So how do we escape the traps or temptations? We must have a relationship with Jesus and submit to authority. Remember, Jesus knows our heart, so we must open our hearts to him and reveal all secret sins, desires, pain, hurts, thoughts, and motivations.

Levels of Authority

In Luke 19:15-26, Jesus relates the parable of the talents where a certain nobleman (Jesus) who went into a far country (heaven) to receive for himself a kingdom *Kingdom of God, and to return, called his ten servants to deliver to each ten pounds (gifts), and said unto them, *"Occupy till I come."* This expression means that the servants of God are to be about the business of the Kingdom. We are to not weary in the service of the Lord knowing he will return and keep accounts. In the parable, the ruler gives each servant a fixed amount to invest. Each servant doubles his investment, except for the third. To the first servant who gained ten pounds, the master (Jesus) gave authority over ten cities. To the second servant who gained five pounds, the master gave him authority over five cities; however, to the third servant, the master rebuked and ordered that the talent be taken and given to the servant who had gained ten talents. In short, this parable is about the return of Jesus Christ and the rewards or levels of authority his faithful servants will receive for their works done on Earth, but the servant who hides his talent or produces no fruit loses his reward. This is a stern warning for believers to be ready for the coming of the Lord Jesus. We each have talents and gifts to be used for the service of the LORD. Let us not hide those talents or gifts out of cowardice or fear.

Similarly, in Mark 13:34-37, Jesus compared himself to the man taking a far journey, who left his house, and gave *authority* to his servants, and to every man his work, and commanded the porter to watch: "*Watch ye therefore: for ye know not when the master of the house cometh, at even, or at midnight, or at the cockcrowing, or in the morning. Lest coming suddenly he find you sleeping. And what I say unto you I say unto all, Watch.*" When Jesus ascended to heaven, he sent His Holy Spirit to distribute gifts, talents, assignments, and authority. As believers, we have authority over the enemy, devils, and diseases, but not all believers are serving or fulfilling the LORD's mandate. Some are asleep, not expecting the return of the master. Therefore, we are to be alert and ready for the return of Jesus.

It is clear in the Bible that those who are faithful with little, will receive more authority in this life and thereafter. Throughout the Bible, we see how faithful servants such as Moses, Elisha, Joshua, Joseph, and David were promoted to higher levels of authority in their lifetime. Everyone is given a little, but *God is a rewarder of those who diligently seek him* (Hebrews 11:6). Thus, the key to obtaining higher levels of authority over devils and diseases is submission to the will and authority of God.

Pride of Life

Magazines, social media, advertisements, and television programs are focused on the desires of this world: the *lusts of the flesh, lusts of the eyes and the pride of life.* What is the pride of life? The pride of life is a haughty or arrogant spirit. The world teaches us that race, position, status, finances, beauty, gender or even sexual orientation should be a source of pride, but according to 1 John 2:16, "*For everything in the world—the lust of the flesh, the lust of the eyes, and the pride of life—comes not from the Father but from the world.* In the Bible, "*pride of life*" means *"pride in our achievements and possessions,"* so pride has to with self-worship or narcissism. N*arcissism* means obsessed with one's own physical appearance or public perception. The word comes from the ancient Greek myth, *Narcissus*, a hunter known for his beauty and pride, who fell in love with his own image.

Youth today self-worship on social media by posting artsy or highly- retouched selfies and lifestyle pictures. In fact, many of the images that we see online have been digitally enhanced or manipulated. In a 2018 Pew Research Center survey, 43 percent of teens feel pressure to only post content which makes them look good to others. [2] This in turn creates mental health issues such as depression, insecurity, unrealistic expectations, and fears. King Solomon warned, *"Pride goes before destruction, and a haughty spirit before a fall"* (Proverbs 16:18). Moreover, pride is an attitude of the heart: *"Out of the heart of men, proceed evil thoughts, adulteries, fornications, murders, thefts, covetousness, wickedness, deceit, lewdness, an evil eye, blasphemy, pride, foolishness. All these evil things come from within and defile a man"* (Mark 7: 21-23). In other words, our own evil thoughts, attitudes, and judgments can defile our spirit and hinder our relationship with the LORD.

Furthermore, the LORD judges the children of pride. For example, in 2 Chronicles 32, we see the LORD's wrath kindled against King Hezekiah for his pride: *"But Hezekiah did not repay according to the favor shown him, for his heart was lifted up; therefore, wrath was looming over him and over Judah and Jerusalem. Then Hezekiah humbled himself for the pride of his heart, so that the wrath of the LORD did not come upon them in the days of Hezekiah."* The LORD is *"longsuffering to us-ward, not willing that any should perish, but that all should come to repentance"* (2 Peter 3:9). Hence, pride brings judgment, but the LORD is willing to forgive those who humble themselves.

[2] "Teens' Social Media Habits and Experiences," Pew Research Center. http://wwwpewresearch.org/internet/2018/11/28/teens-social-media-habits-and-experience/

The Meek Shall Inherit the Earth

In Matthew 5:5, the word "meek" implies humble or gentle of spirit. Jesus' words overturn this world's philosophy and system. In the world's system, the strong and powerful overcome and subdue the weak and lowly. It is Darwin's theory of evolution that only the fittest survive, multiply and prosper, but in the Kingdom of God, the mighty and proud fall, and the humble are exalted, for "*whosoever therefore shall humble himself as this little child, the same is greatest in the kingdom of heaven*" (Matthew 18:4). What does it mean to humble yourself as a little child? It means to take on the lowly position of a small child. A little child depends on its parents to survive and cannot sustain himself; Jesus warns that "*if we do not change and become like little children, we will never enter the kingdom of heaven.*"

Hence, we must submit ourselves to the LORD with a lowly and contrite spirit, for "*The LORD is nigh unto them that are of a broken heart; and saveth such as be of a contrite spirit*" (Psalm 34:18-20). According to the Hebrew lexicon, a *contrite spirit* means a broken or crushed spirit. In Isaiah 57:15, the prophet declares that the "*high and lofty One that inhabiteth eternity* dwells *with him also that is of a contrite and humble spirit, to revive the spirit of the humble, and the heart of the contrite ones."* What a beautiful promise! He also dwells with those who are crushed in spirit.

Meekness also implies self-sacrifice and faithfulness. For example, in Exodus 32: 11-13, we see a universal revolt of the people. The people gathered themselves in a national rebellion against the God of Israel; Moses offered himself as an atonement for the people and was willing to be *"blotted out of God's book,"* if on this condition they may be spared. God refuses the offer but spares the people. Later, in Numbers 12:3, Miriam and Aaron murmured against Moses and questioned his authority, but the LORD heard it, and in a subtext, the LORD described Moses as, *"A very humble man, more humble than anyone else on the face of the earth."* These characteristics are later found in Jesus, *"even as the Son of Man came not to be served but to serve, and to give his life as a ransom for many"* (Matthew 20:28). In John 13:1-17, Jesus washes the feet of his disciples to set an example for them and to teach them meekness and submission, *"I have set you an example that you should do as I have done for you. Very truly I tell you, no servant is greater than his master, nor is a messenger greater than the one who sent him."* Jesus shows us how to serve in meekness and gentleness. Thus, it is not by force, or might that one can attain greatness in the Kingdom, but lowliness and meekness is the key to being great in the Kingdom of God.

If you are guilty of the sin of rebellion, say this prayer:

Heavenly Father,

I yield my body, soul, and spirit to your authority, will and direction for my life. Blot out my transgressions, iniquity, rebellion. Against thee, thee only, have I sinned, and done this evil in thy sight (Psalm 51:4). Behold, thou desirest truth in my inward parts: and in the hidden part thou shalt make me to know wisdom (Psalm 51: 6). Hide thy face from my sins and blot out all mine iniquities (Psalm 51:9). Wash me thoroughly from mine iniquity and cleanse me from my sin (Psalm 51:2). Create in me a clean heart, o God, and renew a right spirit within me (Psalm 51:10). Give me a meek and humble heart and keep back thy servant also from presumptuous sins; let them not have dominion over me: then shall I be upright, and I shall be innocent from the great transgression (Psalm 19:13). Remember not the sins of my youth, nor my transgressions: according to thy mercy remember thou me for thy goodness sake, O LORD. Good and upright is the LORD: therefore, will he teach me in the way. The meek will guide in judgment: and the meek will he teach his way (Psalm 25:7-10). "Search me O God and know my heart: try me and know my thoughts: And see if there be any wicked way in me and lead me in the way everlasting "(Psalm 139:23-24). If there be pride and rebellion in my heart, reveal it to me. Break the pride of my power (Leviticus 26:19) but keep me from destruction. Open the eyes of my understanding and give me wisdom.

You must continually ask God to search your heart regarding pride, rebellion or even self-righteousness. These sins will lead a soul to hell. You must confess and repent immediately; otherwise, you may die in your sins, but God is gracious to forgive you while you are alive.

CHAPTER SEVEN

The Backslider

Return, ye backsliding children, and I will heal your backslidings. Behold, we come unto thee: for thou art the LORD our God. –Jeremiah 3:22

I f you are a backslider, the Lord wants to restore you, *"Return, O faithless sons; I will heal your faithlessness"* (Jeremiah 3:22). You must rededicate your life to the Lord and follow the same steps. However, if you waver after rededicating your life to the Lord, you will be in a worse state than when you started. The following are some scriptures to consider:

"For if, after they have escaped the defilements of the world through the knowledge of our Lord and Savior Jesus Christ, they are again entangled in them and overcome, the last state has become worse for them than the first" –2 Peter 2:20

"For if we go on sinning deliberately after receiving the knowledge of the truth, there no longer

remains a sacrifice for sins, but a fearful
expectation of judgment, and a fury of fire that
will consume the adversaries. Anyone who has set
aside the law of Moses dies without mercy on the
evidence of two or three witnesses. How much
worse punishment, do you think, will be deserved
by the one who has spurned the Son of God, and
has profaned the blood of the covenant by which
he was sanctified, and has outraged the Spirit of
grace?" –Hebrews 10:26-29

God wants to restore our soul. He is more interested in restoring our soul than we are. In fact, we see His patience and great love toward Israel repeatedly. God searches their heart saying: "*Why is this people of Jerusalem slidden back by a perpetual backsliding? They hold fast deceit; they refuse to return*" (Jeremiah 8:5). What is he saying about us? Are we liking these people who *refuse to return* and *slidden back by a perpetual (continual) backsliding?* God is calling you back to a right relationship with Him, but you must repent and turn back from your sin.

Nakedness

The danger of backsliding is that after you have rejected or turned away from God, you no longer have the protection of the Holy Spirit or the covering of the armor. Spiritually, you become naked like Adam and Eve after they ate of the fruit of the tree of knowledge of good and evil. Nakedness is a condition of the soul. In Revelations 3:18, Jesus warns us to be *"clothed in white raiment, and that the shame of thy nakedness does not appear."* The white raiment represents the glory of the father. Adam and Eve were covered in this glory, but after the fall, the glory departed; they died spiritually, and were naked before God. In Revelations 16:15, Jesus warns, *"Blessed is he that watcheth and keepeth his garments, lest he walk naked, and they see his shame."* The garments refer to our new identity in Christ or born-again spirit. When we accept Jesus Christ as our savior, we become *new creatures: "Therefore if any man be in Christ, he is a new creature: old things are passed away: behold, all things are become new"* (2 Corinthians 5:17).

Legal Rights

What happens when we turn away from our blood-bought freedom? If we continue to sin after salvation, we are giving the enemy legal entry into our lives. This is what happened to King Saul. King Saul was anointed by God or filled with the Holy Spirit. When he refused to obey the voice of the Lord, the Holy Spirit departed: *"Now the Spirit of Yahweh departed from Saul and an evil spirit from Yahweh tormented him"* (1 Samuel 16:14-16). David also talks about the condition of the soul in sin:

> *"Such as sit in darkness and in the shadow of*
> *death, being bound in affliction and iron; Because*
> *they rebelled against the words of God, and*
> *condemned the counsel of the most High:*
> *Therefore he brought down their heart with*
> *labour; they fell down, and there was none to*
> *help." (Psalm 107:10)*

The enemy has a legal right to torment and afflict the soul with heavy chains because of rebellion and rejecting Jesus' sacrifice. But the good news is in the following verse:

> *"Then they cried unto the Lord in their trouble, and*
> *he saved them out of their distresses. He brought*
> *them out of darkness and the shadow of death*
> *and broke their bands asunder." (Psalm 107:14).*

Therefore, we must repent of our sins before God and ask Him to restore our soul. If we cry out to Jesus and repent of our sins, he is faithful to forgive us, deliver us from destruction, and bring us out of the darkness. This world is owned and controlled by the power of darkness. Satan is the ruler of this realm, but as children of God, we are the light of this world.

The Prodigal Son

Now, there are three types of backsliders in the Bible. Jesus provides parables or stories to describe each one. The first one is the parable of the lost son. In the story, there is a man with a large estate, a rich man, who had two sons. The youngest son said to his father, *"Father, give me my share of the estate,"* so, the father agrees to this and divides his property between them. *"Not long after that, the younger son got together all he had, set off for a distant country and there squandered his wealth in wild living."* This young man was a son, not a servant; he was living with the father, but he chose to leave the father for the enticements and entrapments of the world. As a young person, you may feel the world has so much to offer, but the truth is, the world's system is meant to trap and enslave you.

After he spent his inheritance, he found a job feeding pigs. In Judaism, the pig represents an unclean animal, and persons who manage such animals may need to ritually purify themselves to be clean. Therefore, this young man, spiritually speaking, was as unclean as the pigs he was feeding. However,

he was still considered a son, so when he came to his senses, he
said,

> *"How many of my father's hired servants have*
> *food to spare, and here I am starving to death! I*
> *will set out and go back to my father and say to*
> *him: Father I have sinned against heaven and*
> *against you. I am no longer worthy to be called*
> *your son: make me like one of your hired servants.*
> *So, he got up and went to his father." –Luke 15:17*

If we go deeper into this parable, we notice that the young man
was starving due to the famine on the land, but he was really
starving spiritually. Once he rejected the father (God), he began
to dry up spiritually and experience a famine. This is what
happened to Adam and Eve after disobeying God and eating the
fruit of the knowledge of good and evil. Their spirits died and as
a result, their connection with the father was severed that very
same day. However, Jesus came to restore that severed cord or
relationship: the key here is repentance. The young man
recognized his sinful condition and repented (*turned around or
reconsidered*).

> *"But while he was still a long way off, his father*
> *saw him and was filled with compassion for him:*

> he ran to his son, threw his arms around him and
> kissed him."—Luke 15:20

If you are a backslider, you must first recognize your sinful
condition, repent, and return to the father. If you do, he will
have compassion on you and restore you.

> "But the father said to his servants, 'Quick! Bring
> the best robe and put it on him. Put a ring on his
> finger and sandals on his feet. Bring the fattened
> calf and kill it. Let's have a feast and celebrate.
> For this son of mine was dead and is alive again;
> he was lost and is found." –Luke 15:22

In thinking about this parable, how many of us have been led
astray by the lust and pride of life. We search for meaning,
purpose and love and find ourselves lost and feeding the pigs. In
other words, we experience a spiritual famine or wilderness. We
do not know how long the young man remained in the world.
For some of us, it may be years. Hearken our souls unto God
before the days grow dim, for in our youth, we think we have
tomorrow, but tomorrow is not promised to us:

> "Come now, you who say, "Today or tomorrow we
> will go to such and such a city, spend a year there,
> buy and sell, and make a profit; whereas you do

not know what will happen tomorrow. For what is your life? It is even a vapor that appears for a little time and then vanishes away." --James 4:13-14

This is a warning to all the youth who think that they have tomorrow, but it is by God's grace that we live and move and have our being, so fear God and keep your souls.

The Lost Sheep

Another type of backslider is pictured in the parable of the lost sheep. In this parable found in John 10:1-18, Jesus heard the Pharisees and scribes murmuring saying, "*This man receiveth sinners, and eateth with them.* And Jesus responds:

> *"What man of you, having a hundred sheep, if he loses one of them, doth not leave the ninety and nine in the wilderness, and go after that which is lost, until he finds it? And when he hath found it, he layeth it on his shoulders, rejoicing." Jesus continues: "I say unto you, that likewise joy shall be in heaven over one sinner that repenteth, more than over ninety and nine just persons, which need no repentance." --John 10:1-8*

According to the *Spurgeon Study Bible* note, the sheep is one of the most foolish creatures. It will wander in any direction leaving the safety of the pasture to the jaws of a wolf and will not instinctively turn away from danger. The sheep will go astray and not know how to return. If it were not for the shepherd, the sheep would be forever lost. In Psalm 23, David depicts the Lord as the good shepherd: *"The Lord is my shepherd; I shall not want. He maketh me to lie down in green pastures: he leadeth me beside the still waters. He restoreth my soul; he leadeth me in the paths of righteousness for his name's sake."* It is the good shepherd (Jesus Christ) who leads us and restores (repairs, refreshes or brings back) our soul. It is through Jesus' sacrifice on the cross that the Lord has redeemed our souls from the *law of sin and death.*

In Judaism, animal sacrifices were required to atone (pay) for the sins of the people. An unblemished sheep according to Jewish law was an acceptable sacrifice or offering to God. The unblemished sheep or lamb is a symbol of Jesus' sacrifice. In John 1:29, John the Baptist declares: *"Behold, the Lamb of God, who takes away the sin of the world."* The sheep here is a reference to believers or those who follow Christ. Hence, the lost sheep is a believer who has lost his way, deceived by false doctrines.

"The hired hand is not the shepherd and does not own the sheep. So, when he sees the wolf coming, he abandons the sheep and runs away. Then the wolf attacks the flock and scatters it. The man runs way because he is a hired hand and cares nothing for the sheep." –John 10:12

The hired man is a type and symbol of the false teacher, priest, or prophet. This man teaches false doctrines and perverts the truth that leads a congregation straight to hell, but Jesus promises to look for the lost sheep of Israel and other sheep too, who are not of this fold: *"I have other sheep that are not of this sheep pen, I must bring them also. They too will listen to my voice and there shall be one flock and one shepherd."* (John 10:16) In other words, if you have been deceived or led astray by false doctrines, pop culture or worldly influences, know that Jesus is looking for you.

In my youth, I was fascinated by the occult. Occult means hidden knowledge; I was fascinated by the afterlife and magic, so I wanted to learn more about these things. I studied *"The Tibetan Book of the Dead"* that describes the soul's journey after death to the underworld. This text offered no hope of a better life after death but depicted the soul's tortured experience in the bowels of the earth. I also read on the teachings of the kabbalah or Jewish mysticism written in the Zohar where I learned about the inner dimensions of reality: the goal was to reach higher elevated meditative states of consciousness through mystical exercises and incantations. One day while I was meditating, in my spirit, I heard, "Anyone entering the Kingdom of heaven must come into it like a child." This was a reference to Mark 10:15: *"Verily I say unto you, whosoever shall not receive the kingdom of God as a little child, he shall not enter therein."* This was a revelation to me because a child does not strive, he simply believes. All the religions of the world teach that to reach Nirvana or paradise, one must work hard and strive, but here, Jesus says that you must simply believe in the one whom God sent. I decided from then on to stop my striving and simply believe.

If you are dabbling in the occult, you may be searching for the truth, but will not find it. In John 14:6 NIV Jesus says, *"I am the way and the truth and the life. No one comes to the Father except through me."* God warns in Genesis 2:7 NIV "but you must not eat of the tree of the knowledge of good and evil, for when you eat from it you will certainly die." The thirst for hidden knowledge can lead us (humanity) in a downward spiral. Our advances in technology and medicine have certainly improved the quality of life on earth but have also led us down the path of destruction. For example, at HAARP Research Facility, a high-power, high-frequency transmitter can now alter weather using a steerable electromagnetic beam super heating the ionosphere or Earth's upper atmosphere. This is the real cause of global warming. SpaceX, governments, and groups like Deep mind are now experimenting with AI autonomous weapons and autonomous-powered algorithms capable of destroying humanity. This occult knowledge has led us to our own destruction.

The Lost Coin

The third type of backslider is described in the parable of the lost coin in Luke 15: 8-10:

> *"Or suppose a woman has ten silver coins and loses one. Does she not light a lamp, sweep the house and search carefully until she finds it? And when she finds it, she calls her friends and neighbors together and says, 'Rejoice with me; I have found my lost coin.' In the same way, I tell you, there is rejoicing in the presence of the angels of God over one sinner who repents."*

The silver coin, like the Roman denarius, was equivalent to a day's wage and represented immense value to the poor. Our souls have immense value in the kingdom of God. According to God, our souls are *"more precious than fine gold."* –Isaiah 13:12; therefore, the enemy *"prowls around like a roaring lion looking for someone to devour."* —1 Peter 5:8. In the spiritual realm, the devil searches to destroy our soul. As discussed in Chapter 1, the soul is the link between our spirit and body. It is the mechanism or device that transmits or translates thoughts, messages from the spirit realm to the physical realm. If the devil can fragment or devour your soul, he can damage the relationship you have with God, for God is a spirit. The lost coin is a believer who has forsaken God for the love of mammon. Mammon is the false god of this world and of deceitful riches. Mammon refers to the desire to pursue of wealth as a primary goal in life. Jesus said, *"No man can serve two masters: for either he will hate the one and love the other; or else he will hold to the one and despise the other. Ye cannot serve God and mammon."* –Matthew 6:24.

Not My Will, But Yours Be Done

Your *will* (*heart*) inclined (*turned*) toward the knowledge of good and evil will bring death and enmity between you and God. In the Isaiah 55:3, it says to *"Incline your ear and come to Me: listen so that your soul may live."* The ear refers to your spiritual ears or inner man. In Judaism, reading aloud and memorizing the Tanakh or Holy Scriptures was a customary practice, so when the Lord gently chides us to incline our ear, He is not talking about our physical ears, but our hearts. We must not only listen but meditate on the Word until it brings about a change of heart. True repentance means changing our habits, attitudes, thoughts, and actions.

God does not force anyone to follow Him. He simply allows every soul to choose. For example, in Deuteronomy 30:15-20, God gives the Jews a choice: life or death and destruction:

> *"But if your heart turns away and you are not obedient, and if you are drawn away to bow down to other gods and worship them, I declare to you this day that you will certainly be destroyed. You will not live long in the land you are crossing the Jordan to enter and possess."*

What does this mean? It means that you must die to yourself: selfish desires and stubborn ways and choose life. This is how you keep your soul. Jesus said:

> *"If any man will come after me, let him deny himself, and take up his cross, and follow me. For whosoever will save his life shall lose it: and whosoever will lose his life for my sake shall find it."* *–Matthew 16:23-25.*

[179]

In the above verse, *"For whosoever will save his life shall lose it"* is not referring to your physical life, but your worldly ambitions or desires, so if you hold on to your *life,* you will lose it. Please understand--discipleship costs everything. For example, When Jesus met Peter, Peter was a simple fisherman. He had to make a choice to follow Jesus and leave his *life* as a fisherman behind. *"'Come, follow me*, Jesus said, *and I will make you fishers of men.'"* –Matthew 4:19 Jesus is telling his disciples that souls are high priority for the kingdom of God. In fact, we are to *"Seek the Kingdom of God above all else, and live righteously, and he will give you everything you need."*—Matthew 6:33.

When we seek after the kingdom, we might have to make sacrifices or give up things. For example, let's say you fell in love, and that person is your soul mate, but they live faraway. What will you do? Will you have a long-distance relationship, or will you give up everything to pursue love? Similarly, Jesus says, *"Everyone who has left houses or brothers or sisters or father or mother or wife or children or fields for my sake will receive a hundred times as much and will inherit eternal life."*—Matthew 19:29. Please understand—Jesus is not saying you should be homeless but be led by His Spirit for the direction of your life. If you are not ready or willing to make sacrifices for Christ, then you are disqualified from serving in the Kingdom: *"No one who puts a hand to the plow and looks back is fit for service in the kingdom of God."*—Luke 9:62. This is serious business.

Many young people today are not ready to take on this kind of commitment because it implies leaving their comfort zone. What is a comfort zone? For most, it means your routines, habits, or daily life, but Jesus is calling us to a purpose-driven life in the Kingdom of God. We were created with a divine calling and assignment, and many in the body are asleep. They wander aimlessly from one event to another trying to find meaning and purpose in life, but the *abundant life* does not mean living for yourself, it means living for Him. Even Jesus Christ in the Garden of Gethsemane submitted to God's will and prayed, *"Father, if you are willing, take this cup from me; yet not my will, but yours be done."*—Luke 22:42. We must be obedient to the will of God even if it costs us our very lives. What does that mean? If the disciples obeyed Jesus unto death or martyrdom, why should we be any different.

In Romans 8:13 KJV, Paul writes, *"For if ye live after the flesh, ye shall die but if ye through the Spirit do mortify the deeds of the body, ye shall live."* We need to submit to the will of the Father rather than our will or desires. In the Lord's prayer Matthew 6:1-13, Jesus models how we should pray: *"Our Father in heaven, hallowed be your name, your kingdom come, your will be done, on earth as it is in heaven.*" It is God's will, not our selfish desires, dreams, and ambitions, to which we should hearken. The world's message is a popular one: *follow your dreams*, but this is a deception because the disciples did not follow their dreams, they followed Christ and as a result, were beaten, tortured, mocked, and executed. We must follow Christ no matter what the cost. This is the true test of our faith.

Obedience is the key to fulfilling God's will. It is only when we agree with God and obey his commands, that we remain in Jesus: *"If you keep my commands you will remain in my love, just as I have kept my Father's commands and remain in his love"* (John 15:10). Jesus warns: *"If anyone does not remain in me, he is thrown aside like a branch and he withers. They gather them, throw them into the fire and they are burned"* (John 15:6).

Do Not Harden Your Heart

There is a warning for the youth: Do not harden your heart like Pharaoh. In Exodus 8:32, we read *"But Pharaoh again became stubborn and refused to let the people go."* Why did Pharaoh become stubborn? As you recall the story of the Exodus, God called Moses to lead his people out of Egypt to the Judean Wilderness. Pharaoh hardened his heart, or did not submit to the will of God, so God brought ten plagues upon the land of Egypt.

The ten plagues represents God judgments on the Egyptian idols worshipped: 1) The Nile River turning to blood was wrath poured on the Egyptian god of the Nile 2) The plague of frogs coming out of the Nile River was against the Egyptian goddess of fertility, water and renewal 3) Lice from the dust of the earth was punishment for the Egyptian god of the Earth 4) Swarms of flies was a pronouncement over the Egyptian god of creation, movement of the Sun, rebirth 5) The death of cattle and livestock was a verdict against the Egyptian goddess of love and protection 6) The plague of boils and sores was vengeance upon Isis—Egyptian goddess of medicine and peace 7) Hail raining down in the form of fire was a sentence on the Egyptian goddess of the sky 8) The plague of locust was retribution for the Egyptian god of storms and disorder 9) Three days of total darkness was punishment on Ra—the Egyptian sun god 10) Death of Egypt's first born was God's judgment on Pharaoh—the ultimate power of Egypt

Pharaoh called on Moses to intreat God's mercy, and Moses and Aaron cried unto the LORD, and the LORD stopped it, but after God removed his hand of judgment upon the land, Pharaoh again hardened his heart. Even after Pharaoh repented of his sin and the judgment of God was lifted, he hardened his heart yet again. We see this in Exodus 9:27-28:

> *"And Pharaoh sent, and called for Moses and*
> *Aaron, and said unto them, I have sinned this time:*
> *the LORD is righteous, and I and my people are*
> *wicked. Intreat the LORD (for it is enough) that*
> *there be no more mighty thundering and hail; and*
> *I will let you go, and ye shall stay no longer."*

Pharaoh seemed sincere and even confessed his sin before the LORD, but his heart was still backslidden and unrepentant. You may seem outwardly sincere in your faith. Dutifully, you may attend church services, do works of charity, attend youth camp meetings, and follow religious rituals, but the LORD looks at your heart. He searches your heart (soul). In Jeremiah 17:10, the LORD says: *"But I, the LORD, search all hearts and examine secret motives. I give all people their due rewards, according to what their actions deserve."* He knows your thoughts and motives, so what will you do? Will you surrender and submit to God's will, or will you harden you heart like Pharaoh? Will you repent because of God's judgment, but then harden your heart again because of God's grace? In Hebrews 10:22:29, we read:

"Let us draw near with a true heart in full assurance of faith, having our hearts sprinkled from an evil conscience, and our bodies washed with pure water. Let us hold fast the profession of our faith without wavering; (for He is faithful that promised;) And let us consider one another to provoke unto love and to good works: Not forsaking the assembling of ourselves together, as the manner of some is; but exhorting one another: and so much the more, as ye see the day approaching. For if we sin willfully after that we have received the knowledge of the truth, there remaineth no more sacrifice for sins, but a certain fearful looking for of judgment and fiery indignation, which shall devour the adversaries. He that despised Moses law died without mercy under two or three witnesses: Of how much sorer punishment, suppose ye, shall he be thought worthy, who hath trodden underfoot the Son of God, and hath counted the blood of the covenant, where with he was sanctified, an unholy thing, and hath done despite unto the Spirit of grace?"

Remember, stubbornness or rebellion is at the heart of witchcraft. You must repent of rebellion and submit to the will of God for your life. The Egyptian gods and goddesses represent idols. You may think to yourself that you do not worship idols but the truth is that the Egyptian gods and goddesses have been replaced by modern idols such as: 1) the god of entertainment, uncontrolled appetites or pleasure 2) the god of technology and convenience 3) the god of deceitful riches and mammon 4) the god of nature and science 5) the god of medicine, drugs and alcohol 6) the god of youthful beauty, fertility and love 7) the god of hidden knowledge or worldly wisdom 8) the god of this age 9) the god of military might, strength and power 10) the god of self and self-reliance.

It is the god of self that is the ultimate ruler in the minds and hearts of this generation and must be defeated. If King David, a man after God's own heart, committed adultery and murder, but repented and prayed to be restored and cleansed, you too can pray to be restored and delivered:

Prayer for the Backslider

Oh Lord, you revive the spirit of the humble, and revive the heart of the contrite ones...You will heal me and lead me. Restore comfort to me. You said in your WORD, "For I will not contend forever, nor will I always be angry; for the spirit would fail before, and the souls which I have made. For the iniquity of his covetousness, I was angry and struck him; I hid and was angry, and he went on backsliding in the way of his heart. I have seen his way and will heal him; I will also lead him and restore comfort to him" (Isaiah 57:16-18 NIV). "Heal me, O Lord, and I shall be healed" (Jeremiah 17:14). O' Lord, take the obstacle out of my way, for thus says the High and Lofty One who inhabits eternity, whose name is Holy: "I dwell in the high and holy place, with him who has a contrite and humble spirit" (Isaiah 57:14-15). You lifted me out of the slimy pit, out of the mud and mire; you set my feet on a rock and gave me a firm place to stand (Psalm 40:2). I will take heed to my ways, that I sin not with my tongue: I will keep my mouth with a bridle, while the wicked is before me. I was dumb with silence, I held my peace, even from good; and my sorrow was stirred. My heart was hot within me, while I was the fire burned. Lord makes me to know mine end, and the measure of my days, what it is; that I may know how frail I am. Behold, thou hast made my days as an handbreath; and mine age is as nothing before thee: verily every man at his best state is altogether vanity. Deliver me from all my transgressions: make me not reproach of the foolish. I was dumb, I opened not my mouth; because thou didst it. Remove thy stroke away from me: I am consumed by the blow of thine hand. When thou with rebukes dost correct man for iniquity, thou makest his beauty to consume away like a moth: surely every man is vanity.

Hear my prayer, O LORD, and give ear unto my cry; hold not thy peace at my tears: for am a stranger with thee, and a sojourner, as all my fathers were. O spare me, that I may recover strength, before I go hence, and be no more (Psalm 39: 1-13). Remember me, O LORD and what you have written about me in your books from the foundation of the world. Thou hast searched me and known me. Thou knowest my downsitting and mine up rising, thou understandest my thought afar off. Thou compassest my path and my lying down, and art acquainted with all my ways. For there is not a word in my tongue, but lo, O LORD, thou knowest it altogether. Thou hast beset me behind and before and laid thine hand upon me. Whiter shall I go from thy spirit? or whither shall I flee from thy presence? If I ascend into heaven, thou art there: if I make my bed in hell, behold, thou art there. If I say, Surely the darkness shall cover me; even the night shall be light about me. Yea, the darkness hideth not from thee; but the night shineth as the day: the darkness and the light are both alike to thee. For thou hast possessed my reins. Search me, O God, and know my heart; try me, and know my thoughts; And see if there be any wicked way in me and lead me in the way everlasting (Psalm 139: 1-24).

CHAPTER EIGHT

Repentance

"Repent therefore, and turn again, that your sins may be blotted out." –Acts 3:19

∽∽∽

R epentance is the key to keeping our soul. We do well to fall on our knees daily and ask Jesus to blot out our transgressions, *"Sanctify us completely and keep our whole spirit, soul and body sound and blameless at the coming of our Lord, Jesus Christ"* (1 Thessalonians 5:23), but the distractions of this world prevent us from having real intimacy with God; and therefore, we nurture guilt, bitterness, unforgiveness in our hearts; it festers and pollutes our soul and spirit. We need to bring our failures, pain, and troubles to Him—the one who created us—to be set free of iniquity and sin. What is iniquity? Iniquity is the old sin nature. After salvation, Jesus begins the work of sanctification through the Holy Spirit in us, but without real repentance, we remain unclean and unworthy to inherit eternal life and enter heaven: *"For of this you can be sure: No immoral,*

impure or greedy person—such a person is an idolater—
has any inheritance in the kingdom of Christ and of God"
(Ephesians 5:5).

Heresies and Lies

Repentance is not guilt or feeling sorry for your actions. It is dying to yourself, saying no to your flesh, and saying yes to God. It is submission; however, *doctrines of devils* are circulating in the church today that proclaim: *"once saved always saved"* or that *"Jesus is love and does not condemn,"* but the reality is much worse, for *" if we deliberately go on sinning after receiving the knowledge of the truth, there no longer remains a sacrifice for sins but a terrifying expectation of judgment and the fury of a fire about to consume the adversaries"* (Hebrews 10:26-27). This means that we could face judgment or die in our sins if we do not repent. To repent means to stop practicing sin or *the works of the flesh*. The Bible never promises eternal salvation. You must kill the flesh, and *"continue to work out your salvation with fear and trembling"* (Philippians 2:12).

The Works of the Flesh

So, what are the *works of the flesh*? In Galatians 5:19-21, *"The works of the flesh are: adultery, fornication, uncleanness, lewdness, idolatry, sorcery, hatred, contentions, jealousies, outburst of wrath, selfish ambitions, dissentions, heresies, envy, murders, drunkenness, revelries, and the like: of which I tell you beforehand, just as I also told you in time past, that those who practice such things will not inherit the kingdom of God.*" This is a warning to the modern church and the youth who "*profess that they know God; but in works they deny him*" (Titus 1:16). Therefore, if we do not repent of the *works of the flesh*, we will NOT enter heaven.

The War Between the Spirit and the Flesh

Paul writes to the church regarding the war between the spirit and the flesh. In Romans 7:24-25, he contends with his own flesh, "*What a miserable man I am! Who will save from this body that brings me death?*" So, the spirit and the flesh oppose each other, but here's the promise, "*if we are led by the Spirit, we are free from the law of sin and death*" (Galatians 5:18). Hence, the *spirit* seeks the Kingdom of Heaven, but the *flesh* seeks to satisfy itself, "*But seek first the Kingdom of God and his righteousness, and all these things will be given to you as well*" (Matthew 6:33). In other words, if we harken to the will of the spirit, we will defeat sin in our lives. We will no longer be a slave to sin.

New Creature

Paul makes a distinction between the carnal and spiritual man, *"But the natural man receiveth not the things of the Spirit of God; for they are foolishness unto him: neither can he know them, because they are spiritually discerned"* (1 Corinthians 2:14 KJV). This is to say that once you are saved and receive the Holy Spirit, you become a *new creature*, and can understand or discern the things of God, *"Therefore if any man be in Christ, he is a new creature: old things are passed away; behold, all things are become new"* (2 Corinthians 5:17 KJV). However, if some *"claim to know God, but by their actions they deny him. They are detestable, disobedient, and unfit for doing anything good"* (Titus 1:16 KJV).

The Work of Sanctification

The Holy Spirit's job is to convict you of sin, but it is your job to repent or turn around. This means that we must deny our flesh and turn from evil. Jesus' blood made atonement for our sins, but the *work of sanctification* is ours. God commands us to sanctify ourselves or make ourselves ready, *"For I am the LORD your God: ye shall therefore sanctify yourselves, and ye shall be holy; for I am holy"* (Leviticus 11:44) and *"For this is the will of God, even your sanctification, that ye should abstain from fornication: That every one of you should know how to possess his vessel in sanctification and honor*" (1 Thessalonians 4:3-7). In Ephesians 5:27, we see the work of sanctification in our lives: "*and to present her to himself as a radiant church, without stain or wrinkle or any other blemish, but holy and blameless.*" This is the picture of the bride of Christ or the body of Christ. We are to appear before Christ holy and blameless without spot or wrinkle. This is the process of purification as the body prepares itself to meet God. In Revelation 19:7, the bride has made herself ready, "*Let us rejoice and be glad and give him glory! For the wedding of the Lamb has come, and his bride has made herself ready.*" This is a powerful image of the work of sanctification in our lives.

Jonah and the City of Nineveh

What does true repentance look like? We see examples of true repentance throughout the Bible, but the most famous was the story of Jonah and the city of Nineveh. Nineveh was an ancient Assyrian city of Upper Mesopotamia located in modern-day Iraq. The Assyrian empire had become extremely great and powerful with Nineveh as its center with over 120,000 people. The Assyrians worshipped Dagon, a fish god, and Ishtar, the fertility goddess, so when Jonah was spewed from the mouth of a fish onto the bank of the river Tigris, the people feared and trembled at the sign. Jonah reluctantly warned the people of impending doom, and as a result, *"the people of Nineveh believed God. They proclaimed a fast and dressed in sack-cloth—from the greatest of them to the least"* (Jonah 3:5). Jesus commended the inhabitants of Nineveh for repenting at the preaching of Jonah, while condemning the Jewish leaders for resisting His message: *"The men of Nineveh will stand up at the judgment with this generation and condemn it; for they repented at the preaching of Jonah, and now something greater than Jonah is here"* (Matthew 12:41).

David and Bathsheba

One of the most tragic stories in the Bible is the story of King David and Bathsheba. David, anointed of God, to lead His people Israel was led astray by his desire. God called King David a man after His own heart. He was known for his mercy, but sadly, David gave the enemy a foothold by coveting (lusting) in his heart. According to Strong's Greek definition, to covet, means to lust after or to set the heart upon that is long for. In other words, David set his heart (longing or desire) upon Bathsheba. We read in 2 Samuel 11 that David arose from off his bed and walked upon the roof of the house and from the roof he saw a woman washing herself; and the woman was incredibly beautiful to look upon. In the Strong's Hebrew dictionary, the word *saw* means to enjoy or experience, gaze, take heed to joyfully look on, spy, stare, consider or regard.

King David, in a moment of weakness, did not turn away his gaze, but continued to spy or joyfully look at Bathsheba's nakedness. He then inquired after the woman and learned that it was the daughter of Eliam, the wife of Uriah the Hittite. And David sent messengers and took her, and came in unto him, and he lay with her; And the woman conceived, and David tried to conceal the pregnancy through deception and then conspired Uriah's death. King David allowed sin to conceive and give birth to death. According to James 1:15, *"Then, when desire has conceived, it gives birth to sin: and sin, when it is full-grown, brings forth death."* Also, in James 4:2 *"You lust and do not have; so, you commit murder. You are envious and cannot obtain; so, you fight and quarrel. You do not have because you do not ask."* After the death of Uriah, David sent and fetched her to his house, and she became his wife and she bore him a son. However, this displeased the LORD, and the LORD sent Nathan unto David. Nathan confronted David, *"Wherefore hast thou despised the commandment of the LORD to do evil in his sight? Thou has killed Uriah the Hittite with the sword, and has taken his wife to thy wife, and hast slain him with the sword of the children of Ammon"* (2 Samuel 12: 9). God rebuked David and warned him of judgment. At this, David acknowledged his sin, *"I have sinned against the LORD."*

We read of David's full repentance in Psalm 51. God was moved by David's repentance and spared his life; however, not without consequences. You see, even though God forgives us of our sins, we cannot escape the consequences of it. Nathan warned David that the sword (death) would never depart from his house (family): *"Now therefore the sword shall never depart from thine house; because thou hast despised me, and hast taken the wife of Uriah the Hittite to be thy wife. Thus, saith the LORD, Behold, I will raise up evil against thee out of thine own house, and I will take thy wives before thine eyes, and give them unto thy neighbor, and he shall lie with thy wives in the sight of this sun. For thou didst it secretly: but I will do this thing before all Israel, and before the sun"* (2 Samuel 12:11-12). The LORD pardoned David but struck the child: *"The LORD also hath put away thy sin; thou shalt not die. And Nathan departed unto his house. And the LORD struck the child that Uriah's wife bare unto David, and it was very sick"* (2 Samuel 12).

David's Repentance Prayer

David's repentance prayer in Psalm 51 is a model prayer that we should follow. David acknowledges God's lovingkindness and asks God to blot out (erase) his transgressions (sins) and wash him of iniquity (weakness or habit). Mosaic law required ritual cleansing for absolution of sin, but David understood, that his heart and spirit had to be cleansed: *"Create in me a clean heart, O god, and renew a right spirit within me"* (Psalm 51:10). To be clean, iniquity or (generational sin) had to be purged and washed: *"Purge me with hyssop, and I shall be clean: wash me, and I shall be whiter than snow"* (Psalm 51:7). David recognizes that his heart (inward parts) needed to change and be restored. He then pleads with God to not abandon or forsake him: *"Cast me not away from thy presence; and take not thy holy spirit from me"* (Psalm 51:11). God had departed from King Saul for disobedience, but God showed mercy to David. Hence, we are not to grieve the Holy Spirit. In short, David humbled himself before the LORD. He cried out and pleaded for mercy.

Baptism of Repentance

John the Baptist preached repentance ahead of the Kingdom of God. You see, one must be born-again in the spirit to enter the Kingdom of Heaven: *"Truly, truly, I say to you, unless one is born of water and the Spirit, he cannot enter the kingdom of God"* (John 3:5). John baptized with water unto repentance (change of heart) and the remission (forgiveness) of sins (Mark 1:4) to prepare the way for the baptism of the Holy Spirit: *"I indeed baptize you with water unto repentance, but He who is coming after me is mightier than I, whose sandals I am not worthy to carry. He will baptize you with the Holy Spirit and fire* (Matthew 9:13). The water baptism, therefore, is symbolic of the new birth. Repentance is the key to the remission (cancellation or forgiveness) of sins. Without the *baptism of repentance*, one cannot enter the Kingdom of God. Even Jesus preached repentance, "From that time on Jesus began to preach, *"Repent, for the kingdom of heaven has come near"* (Matthew 4:17). When Peter preached on the day of Pentecost, he told his listeners to repent (Acts 2:38). In Acts 2:37, the Jews had been "pricked in their heart" by Peter's message. This meant they felt sorrow or grief over their sin; Hence, *"godly sorrow leads to repentance"* (2 Cor. 7:10). However, it is the job of the Holy Spirit to give us repentance that leads to the remission of sins or salvation. In John 6:44, *"No one can come to me unless the Father who sent me draws them, and I will raise them up at the last day."* The Holy Spirit convicts, or declares us guilty of sin, *"And when he comes, he will convict the world of its sin, and of God's righteousness, and of the coming judgment"* John 16:8

NLT. Therefore, it is the Holy Spirit that *pricks our hearts* and baptizes us unto repentance.

Fruits of Repentance

What are the fruits of repentance? Repentance leads to the remission (forgiveness) of sins. John the Baptist told the Jews that they must bring forth *fruit* worthy of repentance (Matthew 3:8). The New Living Translation reads, *"Prove by the way you live that you have repented of your sins and turned to God."* First, we must recognize that we sin against God, himself, *"Against you, you only, have I sinned and done what is evil in your sight, so you are right in your verdict and justified when you judge"* (Psalm 51:4), so we must turn to God for forgiveness knowing He alone can expunge (erase) our record. Second, repentance requires confession (admission) of sins, *"If we confess our sins, he is faithful and just and will forgive us our sins and purify us from all unrighteousness"* (1 John 1:9). Third, repentance requires *works*, *"they should repent and turn to God, and do works befitting for repentance"* (Acts 26:20). This means that after receiving grace (unmerited favor) or forgiveness of sins, we must present ourselves worthy of the gospel, *"Above all you must live as citizens of heaven, conducting yourselves in a manner worthy of the Good News about Christ"* (Philippians 1:27). Thus, we need to live in obedience to the Word of God, *'If you love me, keep my* commands" (John 14:15). Moreover, those who obey the Word of God and do not depart from it, will be rewarded, *"Let us not become weary in doing good, for at the proper time we will reap a harvest if we do not give up"* (Galatians 6:9 NIV).

Baptized in His Death

Once we repent (turn to God), we must not backslide, for we have been baptized in Jesus' death, *"Do you not know that all of us who have been baptized into Christ Jesus were baptized into his death? We were buried therefore with him by baptism into death"* (Romans 6:1). This means that we put to death our old nature, fleshly desires, ambitions, and dreams. We no longer belong to ourselves, but to God, *"Do you not know that your bodies are temples of the Holy Spirit, who is in you, who you have received from God? You are not your own. You were bought at a price"* (1 Corinthians 6:19-20). We have been baptized in Jesus' death, so that we may receive newness of life, *"For if we have united together in likeness of His death, certainly we also shall be in the likeness of His resurrection knowing this, that our old man was crucified with Him, that the body of sin might be done away with, that we should no longer be slaves of sin"* (Romans 6:6). This means that sin no longer has power over us, and neither does death: *"And I give unto them eternal life; and they shall never perish, neither shall any man pluck them out of my hand"* (John 10:28).

Prayer of Repentance:

Have mercy upon me, O God, according to thy lovingkindness: according unto the multitude of thy tender mercies blot out my transgressions. Wash me thoroughly from mine iniquity and cleanse me from my sin. For I acknowledge my transgressions: and my sin is ever before me. Against thee, thee only, have I sinned, and done this evil in thy sight: that thou mightiest be justified when thou speakest, and be clear when thou judgest. Behold, I was shapen in iniquity; and in sin did my mother conceive me. Behold, thou desirest truth in the inward parts: and in the hidden part thou shalt make me to know wisdom. Purge me with your precious blood, and I shall be clean; wash me, and I shall be whiter than snow. Make me to hear joy and gladness; that the bones which thou hast broken may rejoice. Hide thy face from my sins and blot out all mine iniquities. Create in me a clean heart, O God; and renew a right spirit within me. Cast me not away from thy presence; and take not thy holy spirit from me. Restore unto me my soul and the joy of thy salvation; Deliver me from blood guiltiness, O God, thou God of my salvation; and my tongue shall sing aloud of thy righteousness. O Lord open thou my lips; and my mouth shall forth thy praise. For thou desirest not sacrifice; else would I give it: thou delightest not in burnt offering. The sacrifices of God are a broken spirit: a broken and a contrite heart, O God, thou wilt not despise. —Psalm 51:1-17

CHAPTER NINE

The Beginning of Wisdom

The fear of the LORD [is] a fountain of life, to turn [one] away from the snares of death --Proverbs 13:14

In Luke 16: 19-31, Jesus tells the story of the rich man and a poor beggar named Lazarus. Lazarus longed to eat what fell from the rich man's table. The time came when Lazarus died and was carried by the angels to Abraham's side; however, the rich man also died, but he went to hell.

"In torment, the rich man looked up and saw Abraham with Lazarus by his side, so he called to him, 'Father Abraham, have pity on me and send Lazarus to dip the tip of his finger in water and cool my tongue, because I am in agony in this fire.'

"But Abraham replied, 'Son, remember that in your lifetime you received your good things, while Lazarus received bad things, but now he is comforted here, and you are in agony. And besides all this, between us and you a great chasm has been set in place, so

[205]

that those who want to go from here to you cannot, nor can anyone cross over from there to us.'

"He answered, 'Then I beg you, father, send Lazarus to my family, for I have five brothers. Let him warn them, so that they will not also come to this place of torment.'

"Abraham replied, 'They have Moses and the Prophets: let them listen to them.'

"No, father Abraham,' he said, 'but if someone from the dead goes to them, they will repent.'

"He said to him, 'If they do not listen to Moses and the Prophets, they will not be convinced even if someone rises from the dead.'"

This frightening parable teaches us that there are only two places or destinations after death: hell, or paradise. Many modern churches today are not preaching about hell because it is not a popular teaching, yet *the fear of Lord is the beginning of wisdom"* *(Proverbs 9:10).* In Luke 12:5, it reads, *"But I'll tell you whom to fear. Fear God, who has the power to kill you and then throw you into hell. Yes, he's the one to fear."*

It is interesting to note that God, in his infinite mercy and compassion, raised the dead to testify to the truth. For example,

Jesus raised Lazarus from the dead (John 11:25). Jesus also raised the son of a widow (Luke 7:11-17) and Jairus's daughter (Mark 5:21-43). At Jesus' death, there was an earthquake and graves were opened. The dead came back to life and testified to the truth (Matthew 27:51-53):

> "Then behold, the veil of the temple was torn in two from top to bottom, and the earth quaked, and the rocks were split, and the graves were opened; and many bodies of the saints who had fallen asleep were raised; and coming out of the graves after His resurrection, they went into the holy city and appeared to many."

Our merciful God continues to raise the dead to testify to the truth. Many people today have had near-death experiences and have recorded their experiences in books, documentaries, art, and videos. These testimonies serve as first-hand accounts of real afterlife experiences. Many recall in vivid detail the stench, the screams and even the fires of hell. Some have even recorded their visions or experiences in paintings and monuments.

Hell, or Sheol

Many people today deny the existence of hell, but despite what pop culture tries to sell us, the Bible is very clear--Hell is a real place with many regions. For example, in Matthew 24:51, *"He will cut him to pieces and assign him a place with hypocrites, where there will be weeping and gnashing of teeth."* The *"place with the hypocrites"* is a section in hell reserved for the sin of hypocrisy or double mindedness. The *weeping* and *gnashing of teeth* are the punishment of the wicked. Another example is found in Matthew 22:13, *"Bind him hand and foot, and throw him into outer darkness; in that place there will be weeping and gnashing of teeth."* Outer darkness is a real place in hell reserved for demons and those who reject God. In Matthew 5:22, the sins of anger and cursing can bring God's judgment:

> *"But I tell you that anyone who is angry with a brother or sister will be subject to judgment. Again, anyone who says to a brother or sister, 'fool' is answerable to the court. And If you curse someone, you are in danger of the fires of hell."*

Therefore, those who curse, and rage will also be bound and thrown into the *fires of hell*. That is why the enemy works hard to stir up strife, anger, and offense, for he knows that anger and unforgiveness are a one-way ticket to hell. Another region mentioned is the bottomless pit. The bottomless pit is reserved for the very wicked and fallen angels, *"He opened the shaft of the bottomless pit, and from the shaft rose smoke like the smoke of a great furnace."* (Revelations 9:2) Also, the prophet Isaiah writes of men who rebelled against God, *"For their worm shall not die, their fire shall not be quenched, and they shall be an abhorrence to all flesh."* (Isaiah 66:24) The *worm* and *fire* are punishments in hell for those who deny God.

According to the Bible, the location of hell or Sheol is in the center of the Earth. King David references the location of Sheol, *"Let death steal over them; let them go down to Sheol alive; for evil is in their dwelling place and in their heart."* (Psalm 55:15). In Proverbs 7:27, Solomon writes, "Her house is the way to Sheol, going down to the chambers of death." referring to the house of the prostitute or adulterous woman. The depths of hell extend to the lowest parts of the earth. In Isaiah 14:15, the prophet writes, *"But you are brought down to Sheol, to the far reaches of the pit."*

Cultures from around the world believe in hell. The Buddhist, for example, believe in the ten courts of hell and punishment for evildoers. The Greeks, Romans, Egyptians, Hindus, and Tibetan all have revelations of hell or the underworld. For example, the *"The Egyptian Book of the Dead"* describes the various tortures and passages of the underworld. These accounts or depictions of hell are universally all the same. It is a place of endless agony and torture of souls with no escape.

The Fear of God is the Beginning of Wisdom

Fearing God is the beginning of wisdom. If God is love, why should you fear Him? The Bible says in Matthew 10:28 *"Do not be afraid of those who kill the body but cannot kill the soul. Rather, be afraid of the One who can destroy both soul and body in hell."* God is the only one who has the power to determine your fate or destiny. Today, many young people have this false perception that they are the masters of their destiny or control their fate. This is a lie straight from the pit of hell. In the Book of Ecclesiastes 8:7, Solomon, the wisest man to ever live, wrote *"Yet no one knows what will happen because who can tell him what will happen?"* People are desperate to know the future, but no one can predict it except the Lord. He knows the beginning from the end and can accurately predict future events. Therefore, if we cannot predict the future, who can tell us if we live or die tomorrow. James 4:14 reads: *"Why, you do not even know what will happen tomorrow. What is your life? You are a mist that appears for a little while and then vanishes."* In other words, we have absolutely no control of our bodies, in life or death. Despite this glaring truth, many youths arrogantly boast about tomorrow. They do not know or fear God, so they live their lives as though they will live forever, but James 4:13-14 writes:

"Come now, you who say, 'Today or tomorrow we will go to such a city, spend a year there, buy and sell, and make a profit;" whereas you do not know what will happen tomorrow. For what is your life? It is even a vapor that appears for a little time and then vanishes away."

God's mercy is patient and long-suffering with us; however, we do not know what will happen tomorrow, so fear God for it is the beginning of wisdom and a fountain of life.

The Great White Throne Judgement

The dead in Christ, who die without a relationship with Christ, will be judged by Him at the great white throne judgement. John sees the spiritually dead, small, and great, stand before His throne to be sentenced: *"Then I saw a great white throne and him who sat on it...And I saw the dead, small and great, standing before God"* (Revelation 20:11-12). The white throne judgment speaks of the purity and holiness of Jesus, and His worthiness to sit and judge humanity. It was the shed blood of Christ that redeemed us from the pit and unto salvation. It is only fitting that He sits as ruler and judge of all. In fact, Jesus' own words reveal that the Father judges no one, but all power and authority have been given to the Son: *"The Father judges no one but has committed all judgment to the Son...and has given Him authority to execute judgment also, because He is the Son of Man"* (John 5:22, 27). The dead will be called from death and Hades to stand before the Judge of all the earth, and the books will be open, *"The dead were judged according to what they had done as recorded in the books"* (Revelation 20:12). Those who die without Jesus will be judged according to their misdeeds on Earth. In other words, they will be judged (punished) according to their actions while on earth, and another book was opened— the book of life. This is the lamb's book of life, *"And whosoever was not found written in the book of life was cast into the lake of fire* (Revelation 20:15). This is the tragic end for those whose name was blotted out of the book of life.

It is possible for one's name to be blotted out. In Revelations 3:5, Jesus declared, *"He that overcometh, the same shall be clothed in white raiment; and I will not blot out his name out of the book of life."* This suggests that some Christians would not overcome the temptations of the last days, and their names would be blotted (erased) from the lamb's book of life. Jesus is not mincing words here: believers who do not pass the test, will go to the lake of fire.

The Lake of Fire and the Second Death

The lake of fire is a place in hell reserved for the devil and his angels, *"depart from Me into the eternal fire prepared for the devil and his angels"* (Matthew 25:41); however, it is also reserved for those who practice sin and reject Jesus. In Revelation 21:8, John describes their fate: *"But the fearful (cowardly), and unbelieving, and the abominable (vile), and murderers, and whoremongers (sexually immoral), and sorcerers (those who practice magic arts, witchcraft), and idolaters, and all liars, shall have their part in the lake which burns with fire and brimstone: which is the second death."* There are those who ask why God would create such a place, and the answer is clear: God is just. Everyone has been given free will to choose life or death, but *"the soul that sinneth, it shall die"* (Ezekiel 18:20). Therefore, God says, *"I have set before you life and death, blessing and cursing: therefore, choose life"* (Deuteronomy 30:19). Please understand that God requires holiness and purity. In fact, Paul warned the church at Corinth:

> *"Know you not that the unrighteous (wicked) shall not inherit the Kingdom of God? Be not deceived (fooled): neither fornicators (sexually immoral or sex outside marriage), nor idolaters (worship idols), nor adulterers (those who have sex with*

[213]

other people after they are already married), nor

effeminate (men acting like women), nor

homosexuals (those who have sex with the same

sex and break God's law) nor thieves (people who

steal), nor covetous (those greedy for what

belongs to others), nor drunkards (people who

stay intoxicated), nor slanderers (those who speak

bad about others), nor swindlers (people who

deceive others for money), will inherit the Kingdom

of God. Such were some of you, but you were

washed, but were sanctified, but you were justified

in the name of the Lord Jesus Christ and in the

Spirit of our God," (1 Corinthians 6:9-11).

Hence, those who practice sin will die the second death. This is a warning to all the youth who have been indoctrinated by this world system to believe that there are no consequences for sin, or that there is no right or wrong, but the Bible warns, *"And whosoever was not found written in the book of life was cast into the lake of fire"* (Revelation 20:15). Even those who had been washed clean of their sins but backslide *"as a dog returns to its vomit, so a fool repeats his foolishness"* (Proverbs 26:11), will be endanger of losing their soul forever. There is a heresy in the church that *"once saved always saved"* but the truth is *"he that* commits (practices) sins is of the devil" (1 John 3:7-8). In other words, salvation is conditional. If you overcome temptation and resist sin, you will live, "*He who overcomes shall be clothed in white garments, and I will not blot out his name from the Book of Life; but I will confess his name before My Father and before His angels" (Revelation 3:5).* In short, if you continue to practice sin after your initial salvation, your name will be blotted out (removed) from the Book of Life.

How do we keep our souls? God does not want anyone to die, "*but is patient toward us, not willing that any should perish but that all should come to repentance (turn from sin to obedience to God or reconsider)* 2 Peter 3:9. We are to turn away from our sins by denying our flesh pleasure, impulse, or habit. Obedience is the key.

Mark of The Beast

In Revelation 13, John is given a vision of the end times. He sees a *beast* rise out of the *sea*. The *beast has seven heads and ten horns* that resembles a *leopard* with the feet of a *bear* and mouth of a *lion*, and the *dragon*, Satan, gave him its power, and authority to rule on Earth. John's vision is like the prophet Daniel's vision of the large statue with a head of gold, chest and arms of silver, stomach and hips made of bronze, legs of iron and feet of iron and clay. The metals represent kingdoms of the world. Similarly, the beasts in John's vision represent kingdoms of the world that offer their sovereignty or power to the *beast*. It gave power over all nations. In Romans 13:1 NLT, Paul confirms that all authority comes from God:

> *"Everyone must submit to governing authorities. For all authority comes from God, and those in positions of authority have been placed there by God."*

However, the *beast's* power comes from Satan, not God; Therefore, men should not submit to its authority or will.

In Revelations 13:5-16, this *beast* will open its mouth and curse God, his name and heaven. It will make war with the Christians to *overcome* them. This means that Christians will not readily submit to the dragon's authority, and will be persecuted, arrested, and even killed. Then, another beast that exerciseth all the power of the first beast before him, rises out of the *earth* to *deceive* the nations, and causes all:

> *"Both small and great, rich and poor, free and bond, to receive a mark in Their right hand, or in their foreheads: And no man might buy or sell,*

save he that had the mark, or the name of the
beast, or the number of his name."

In Revelation 14:9-11, an angel proclaimed, *"That if any many*
worship the beast and his image, and receive his mark in his
forehead, or in his hand" he will be thrown in the lake of fire and
"they have no rest day nor night, who worship the beast and his
image, and whosoever receiveth the mark of his name."

This is a warning to the youth; you will be *tempted or deceived* to
take the mark or *digital tattoo* for its many benefits:

First, the mark will be a global digital ID microchip with
vaccination, bank, and medical records. Cash and credit card
transactions will be eliminated. You will be required to scan your
hand or forehead to buy, sell or travel eliminating the need for
passports, driver's license, or other forms of identification. Your
chip will also have a tracking device much like your cell phone. It
will monitor your every move. This may be appealing for many
youths who enjoy tracking their loved ones on social media.
Many tech savvy young people will love the convenience and
safety of a cashless society, and the bonus of no proof of
documentation when traveling abroad. On the other hand, this
microchip will track your buying and spending habits, monitor
your behavior and movements, and take away your freedom and

privacy much like the facial recognition 5G technology implemented in China. Anyone who does not comply with the government or ruling class will be punished with a low social credit score, loss of privileges and freedoms. Anyone who refuses the mark will be banished from society.

Second, the chip will be an attractive gizmo or gadget that allows for brain machine interfacing. AI-powered brain interface technology could potentially make people smarter, improve memory and process information more efficiently. This 5G or 6G technology would make it possible to upload information directly to the brain, and even allow gamers to interface with virtual reality. This will be a selling point; however, the reality is that this technology may cause potential side effects such as memory loss or brain damage. This weaponized technology can also be used for mind control or brain hacking. According to an MIT Media Lab report published Dec 2018, *"How to Remote Control a Human Being,"* GVS or galvanic vestibular stimulation can be used to control a person's movement, emotions, and thoughts. This may sound like a fun game, but this would take away your autonomy and individual rights.

Third, the microchip contains nanotechnology and a self-healing hydrogel, or a specialized type of polymer with elastic, flesh-like properties that have been used in tissue reconstructive surgery. This technology will be lauded by the medical and scientific community for its healing properties. It is interesting to note, that in Revelation 9:6, *"And in those days shall men seek death, and shall not find it; and shall desire to die, and death shall flee from them."* The self-healing properties of this technology will cause people to live longer. This will be a major selling point, and even deceive many Christians; however, DO NOT BE DECEIVED! Anyone who worships the beast and his image, and receives his mark in his forehead, or in his hand, shall receive punishment according to Revelation 14:10-11:

> *"The same shall drink of the wine of the wrath of God, which poured out without mixture into the cup of his indignation; and he shall be tormented with fire and brimstone in the presence of the holy angels, and in the presence of the Lamb: And the smoke of their torment ascendeth up for ever and ever; and they have no rest day nor night, who worship the beast and his image, and whosoever receiveth the mark of his name."*

In short, the *mark* will be touted as a new technology with many advantages and privileges but will be a means to control people. The chip will be mandatory, and those who refuse it will be breaking the law and considered terrorists or criminals. They will

[219]

be marginalized, ridiculed, and persecuted. However, whoever takes the mark will burn in the lake of fire for all eternity. Therefore, you must refuse the mark unto death, the Bible says,

> *"And fear not them which kill the body, but are not able to kill the soul, but rather fear him which is able to destroy both soul and body in hell"* *(Matthew 10:28).*

> *"For whoever wants to save their life will lose it, but whoever   loses their life for me will find it"* *(Matthew 16:25).*

Prayer to Escape the Wrath of God:

Father keep me from the hour of judgment. Spirit of deception, the Lord rebuke you. The spirit of truth, Holy Spirit, deliver your people from spiritual blindness and deafness. Take the veils off my eyes and ears. Cleanse me of all unrighteousness and iniquity. I repent of evil thoughts, sexual immorality, theft, adultery, lying, slander, pride, selfishness, covetousness, idol worship and uncleanness. Forgive me for practicing magical arts, perversion, idolatry, and falsehood. Wash me of malice, murmuring, complaining, walking after my own lusts, and speaking vain and idle words. I reject the world's influence, pleasures, and enticements. I aim to please you and not man.

Your WORD declares, "The fear of man bringeth a snare: but whoso putteth his trust in the LORD shall be safe (Proverbs 29:25). I care not about myself, my body or creature comforts, but I commit my body, soul, mind, and spirit to your will.

Give me the courage to face hardships and trials for your name's sake. I will overcome just as you overcame the world. For your WORD declares, "That in me ye might have peace. In the world ye shall have tribulation; but be of good cheer, I have overcome the world" (John 16:33). I will not be a friend of the world, for your Word says in James 4:4, "You adulterers! Don't you realize that friendship with the world makes you an enemy of God?" Deliver me from your wrath and keep me hidden in your secret place. Remember me, LORD. Write my name in the palms of your hands and intervene on my behalf. Destroy my enemies and keep watch over my soul. Preserve my whole spirit, soul, and body at the coming our Lord, Jesus Christ (1 Thessalonians 5:21) Hold me up with your victorious right hand (Isaiah 41:10). Amen

CHAPTER TEN

Identity and Purpose in Christ

"So, God created man in his own image, in the image of God he created him; male and female he created them." –
Genesis 1:27

Y ou were made in the image of God. What does that mean? Your spirit (divine nature), soul (thoughts, emotions) and body (physical attributes) were made(fashioned) to reflect the Godhead. In Ephesians 5:1-5, Paul writes to the church that we are to be *"imitators of God walking in love just as Christ loved us and gave Himself up for us."* If we want to have victory over the enemy, we must conform to the image of Christ. We must put away impurity, immorality, greed, silly talk, filthy language. We are to seek after righteousness, holiness, and meekness. We must arise from our slumber and seek after the Lord. The Lord says, *"Therefore be careful how you walk, not as unwise men but as wise, making the most of your time, because the days are evil."* –Ephesians 5:15. If you are seeking after entertainment, pleasure or riches, the Lord is telling you to arise from the dead (spiritual sleep), or to wake up because time is short, and the times are evil.

Don't Believe the Lie

Many youths are asleep because they don't know their identity or purpose in life, so they are caught up *"like the churning of the sea that can't keep still. They churn up from their waters muck and mud." –Isaiah 57:20* The waters are a reference to their inner man or heart. An unclean heart will produce "muck and mud." In Proverbs 4:23, David writes, *"Guard your heart above all else, for it determines the course of your life."* Many young people have rejected the truth (Jesus) to bow down to the gods of *pop culture and political correctness.* They have allowed the *world system* to define who they are and so have believed a lie. For example, some youths now self-identify as non-binary, trans or part of the LGTBQ+ community, but these *labels* should not define the individual. Gender dysphoria is part of the great deception of the last days: *"They perish because they did not accept the love of the truth and so be saved. For this reason, God sends them a strong delusion so that they will believe the lie and so that all will be condemned who have not believed the truth but have delighted in wickedness* (2 Thessalonians 2:11-17). In other words, those who reject Jesus and his commandments, will believe a lie. Hence, there are cases of people who have believed the lie about their identity and have proceeded with gender reassignment surgery only to find out months, years later that it was a mistake. Still, others believe they are alcoholics, drug addicts, etc.... and feel helpless to change. These *labels* are really meant to deceive you. You see, the dark rulers of this world are doing everything they can to convince you that you were not made in the image of God, but rather, a product of evolution, an accident or mistake of nature. But in fact, it is God himself who created you: *"For it was you who created my inward parts; you knit me together in my mother's womb"* (Psalm 139:13). The truth is that God created us to be His children, from the foundation of the world: *"For he chose us in him before the creation of the world to be holy and blameless in his sight. In love"* (Ephesians 1:4). So how do we remain blameless in his sight? How do we remain in his love?

We must first repent and acknowledge our sins before the Lord, and then we must be filled with the Holy Spirit (living waters). We must also develop and maintain a relationship with the Father and seek after Him. To develop a relationship with the Father, we must read the Word and ask the Holy Spirit to help us reveal its truth. We must also understand our identity in Christ that we were made in the image of God. Then, we must surrender to Him and deny ourselves. We must stop seeking after worldly pursuits, but *"Seek the Kingdom of God above all else, and live righteously, and he will give you everything you need."* (Matthew 6:33)

Let Us Make Man in Our Image

To better understand God's plan and purpose for us, we must go back to the beginning. In Genesis 1:26-27, we see that God said,

> *"Let us make man in our image, after our likeness: and let them have dominion over the fish of the sea, and over the fowl of the air, and over the cattle, and over all the earth, and over every creeping thing that creepeth upon the earth. So, God created man in his own image, in the image of god created he him; male and female created he them."*

Hence, we were originally created to have dominion (sovereignty or control) over the earth and to reflect God's nature and glory, but after the fall, dominion was given to Satan and the fallen angels: *"And the devil, taking him up into an high mountain, shewed unto him all the kingdoms of the world in a moment of time. And the devil said unto him. All this power will I give thee, and the glory of them: for that is delivered unto me; and to whomsoever I will I give it"* (Luke 4:5-6).

Adam and Eve lost their original *glory* and stood naked before God: *"Then the eyes of both of them were opened, and they realized they were naked; so, they sewed fig leaves together and made coverings for themselves"* (Genesis 3:7). Nakedness is usually associated with shame and sin throughout the Bible: For example, Exodus 28: 42,43, the LORD orders that the priests are to be covered, *"Make for them linen undergarments to cover their naked bodies; they must cover from the waist to the thighs. These must be on Aaron and his sons when they enter to the tent of meeting, or when they approach the altar to minister in the Holy Place, so that they bear no iniquity and die."* In the Book of Revelations, Jesus warns the church: *"I counsel thee to buy of me gold tried in the fire, that thou mayest be rich; and white raiment, that thou mayest be clothed, and {that} the shame of thy nakedness do not appear; and anoint thine eyes with eye salve, that thou mayest see"* (Revelations 3:18). To be clothed in white raiment is to be sanctified (set apart, holy) by the blood of Christ. White symbolizes purity and holiness. Therefore, the High Priests who served in the temple wore white garments on the Day of Atonement or Day of Judgment. Meaning, we too, must be dressed in white garments (purified) on the Day of Judgment.

[227]

In short, we were made in the image of God. We are carriers of his glory. This means we are to be *clothed* (covered) in white raiment (holiness) or born again in the spirit through our confession in Christ who redeems us from sin and death. Jesus not only restored our authority but covered our nakedness (shame). We are born of *spirit and water*, and the glory of God, now lives inside of us.

Becoming One with the Lord

Our true purpose is to become one with God just as Jesus is one with the father. We are to become one in the spirit, so that our actions, thoughts, and emotions reflect the father. In John 17:20-23, Jesus prayed not only for his disciples, but those who would believe on Him:

That they all may be one; as thou, Father, art in me, and I in thee, that they also may be one in us: that the world may believe that thou hast sent me. And the glory which thou gavest me I have given them; that they may be one, even as we are one: I in them, and thou in me, that they may be made perfect in one; and that the world may know that thou hast sent me, and hast loved them, as thou has loved me.

Do you understand what Jesus was praying? We have direct access to His glory when we are baptized with the Holy

Spirit, but there are levels of glory. Our purpose in this world is to be *made perfect in one* to reflect the *full measure* of His glory, so that the world may know the truth. This is not referring to the ecumenical movement or effort to join all denominations and religions of the world into one, but it does mean, individually and corporately as a body, to strive toward perfection (holiness and love) in Jesus. It means to die to self completely, so that we are joined in spirit, soul, and body to the Godhead: *"Now may the God of peace himself sanctify you completely. And may your whole spirit, soul and body be kept sound and blameless at the coming of our Lord Jesus Christ"* (1 Corinthians 5:23). It is hard to imagine how this can be possible but think of it as a marriage between a husband and wife. According to the Jewish tradition, when a husband and wife enter covenant, they become one flesh. This is how God sees the covenant of marriage. Therefore, when we enter a covenant (relationship) with the Godhead, we become one spirit: *"But he that is joined unto the Lord is one spirit"* (1 Corinthians 6:17).

Meditations and Prayers to Restore Identity

1. God made me and recorded it in His book.

> *"For thou hast possessed my reins: thou hast covered me in my mother's womb. I will praise*

thee; for I am fearfully and wonderfully made marvelous are thy works; and that my soul knoweth right well. My substance was not hid from thee, when I was made in secret, and curiously wrought in the lowest parts of the earth. Thine eyes did see my substance yet being unperfect; and in thy book all my members were written, which in continuance were fashioned, when yet there was none of them" (Psalm 139:13-16).

2. God delivered me out of the womb.

"But thou art he that took me out of the womb: thou didst make me hope when I was upon my mother's breasts. I was cast upon thee from the womb: thou art my God from my mother's belly" (Psalm 22:9-10).

"Shall I bring a baby to the point of birth and not deliver it?" says the LORD. "Or will I who deliver close the womb?" says your God" (Isaiah 66:9).

3. God formed me and knows all my ways.

"Before I formed you in the womb, I knew you, before you were born I set you apart" (Jeremiah 1:5).

"O LORD, You have searched me and known me. You know my sitting down and my rising up; You understand my thought afar off. You comprehend my path and my lying down, And are acquainted with all my ways. For there is not a word on my tongue, But behold, O LORD, You know it altogether" (Psalm 139: 1-4).

4. God thinks about me.

"How precious also are thy thoughts unto me, O God! How great is the sum of them! If I should count them, they are more in number than the sand: when I awake, I am still with thee." (Psalm 139:1-18).

5. God made me in His image.

"For we are God's masterpiece. He has created us anew in Christ Jesus, so we can do the good things he planned for us long ago" (Ephesians 2:10).

"So, God created man in his own image, in the image of God created he him: male and female created he them" (Genesis 1:27).

6. God loves me.

"I have loved you with an everlasting love" (Jeremiah 31:3 NIV).

"He heals the brokenhearted and binds up their wounds' (Psalm 147:3).

'See what kind of love the Father has given to us, that we should be called children of God; and so, we are. The reason the world does not know us is that it did not know him" (1 John 3:1).

7. God chose me from the beginning.

"You didn't choose me, remember; I chose you, and put you in the world to bear fruit, fruit that won't spoil. As fruit bearers, whatever you ask the Father in relation to me, he gives you" (John 15:16).

"But we are bound to give thanks to God always for you, brethren beloved by the LORD, because

God from the beginning chose you for salvation through sanctification by the Spirit and belief in the truth" (2 Thes 2:13).

8. God made me a King and Priest.

"But you are a chosen people, a royal priesthood, a holy nation, God's special possession "(1 Peter 2:9 NIV).

"And hath made us kings and priests unto God and his Father; to him be glory and dominion for ever and ever. Amen" (Revelation 1:6).

9. God remembers me.

"See, I have written your name on the palms of my hands" (Isaiah 49:16).

Prayer to Restore Proper Identity

O' Lord, have mercy on me. Show me your lovingkindness. Blot out my sins and wash me clean of all iniquity (generational or habitual sins). With a broken spirit, I confess all my secret sins - (be specific of sins) and give me the power to overcome them through your Holy Spirit. Today, restore my soul and align my personality, mind, thoughts, and emotions with your Word. Heal my heart, soul and spirit of any word curses, physical and mental abuse, or trauma I have suffered. Take out any demonic weapons, daggers, spears from my spirit and destroy all wicked covenants, word curses over my life and soul. I release - (name of person or people who hurt you; if you don't remember their names, try to remember their faces) of any wrongdoing and lay it on the altar. I forgive and release all those who afflicted my soul. You say, love your enemies and pray for those who persecute you (Matthew 5:44), so I pray for those souls who have bullied, hurt, and rejected me that they may repent of their sins and be saved.

Your Word declares that whatever I bind on earth will be bound in heaven; and whatever I loose on earth will be loosed in heaven (Matthew 18:18), so I bind any spirit of manipulation, rebellion, idolatry, witchcraft, fear, rejection, anger, confusion, double-mindedness, deception, sexual perversion, root of bitterness and a reprobate mind to be cast into the abyss, and I loose the angelic host to war and defeat my enemies (dark rulers) and the windows of heaven to pour out blessings, joy and peace on me. I close any open gates or portals of the enemy and invite your Holy Spirit to live with me. Father, you are not the author of confusion but of peace (1 Corinthians 14:33), so take away the spirit and author of confusion and bring peace to my mind and heart. You have not given us over to fear and confusion, but of power and love and of a sound mind (2 Timothy 1:7). Today, - (date) I make a covenant to serve you Jesus. I submit my spirit, soul and body to your will and let my whole spirit, soul and body be kept sound and blameless at your coming (1 Thessalonians 5:23). Sanctify and clothes me with righteousness. You say "For my thoughts are not your thoughts neither are your ways my ways (Isaiah 55:8), so help me to think your thoughts and establish my ways in the TRUTH. Make a level path for my feet and make my way sure (Proverbs 4:26).

DECLARE:

LORD, I praise you because I am fearfully and wonderfully made; my substance was not hid from you when I was made in secret, and all my members (body parts) were recorded in your book. You knew me before you formed me in my mother's womb, and you set me apart. You chose me from the beginning to be saved and sanctified. You love me with an everlasting love; You healed my broken heart, restored my soul, and closed my wounds. I am a child of God because you offered your only son as a sacrifice in exchange for my soul; the world does not know me because they did not know you. I am a special possession made in the image of God and created anew in Jesus Christ.

Remember to keep your vows!

CHAPTER ELEVEN

The Narrow Gate

"Enter by the narrow gate; for wide is the gate and broad is the way that leads to destruction, and there are many who go in by it." –Matthew 7:13

I n Matthew 7:13, Jesus tells his followers to "Enter through the narrow gate. For wide is the gate and broad is the road that leads to destruction, and many enter through it. But small is the gate and narrow the road that leads to life, and only a few find it." Here, Jesus points to two gates in which a soul will enter: the narrow gate or the wide gate. Notice that the road or path that leads to the wide gate is inclusive, but the life path that leads to the small gate is very exclusive and only a few find it. What does this mean? This means that very few Christians will be saved.

According to a 2015 Pew Research Center survey there are 2.3 billion Christians around the world, * so to put it into perspective, out of 2.3 billion so-called Christians, only a *few* will enter the Kingdom of Heaven. The *NAS Exhaustive Concordance* defines *few* as a remnant or survivors. In Romans 9:27, Isaiah prophesizes concersea; Israel: "*Though the number of the children of Israel be as the sand of the sea, the remnant will be saved.*" So, who are the remnant?

In Revelations 12:17KJV, the remnant are those "*which keep the commandments of God, and have the testimony of Jesus Christ.*" The remnant are the wise virgins (Jesus 'followers) who brought enough oil for their lamps and were prepared for the bridegroom's arrival, while the foolish virgins (carnal Christians), were left behind and disowned (Matthew 25:1-13). Hence, the bridegroom is Jesus, and the virgins are the church members. There are those in the church who are not prepared or ready for Jesus' visitation. In Luke 19:44, Jesus prophesied to the Jews saying, "*And shall lay thee even with the ground, and thy children within thee; and they shall not leave in thee one stone upon another because thou knewest not the time of thy visitation.*" The Jews rejected Jesus as their Messiah.

Similarly, there are many Christians today who do not discern the sign of the times. Jesus warned his followers of the signs of His eminent return. In Matthew 24:3-13, the disciples asked Jesus, "*What will be the sign of Your coming, and of the end of the age?* Jesus described the terrible persecution and trials for the church body:

> *"Then shall they deliver you up to be afflicted and*
> *shall kill you: and ye shall be hated of all nations*
> *for my name's sake. And then shall many be*
> *offended, and shall betray one another, and shall*
> *hate one another. And many false prophets shall*
> *rise and shall deceive many. And because iniquity*
> *shall abound, the love of many shall wax cold. But*
> *he that shall endure unto the end, the same shall*
> *be saved."*

These verses are for the last days' church. Many in the church will be persecuted, offended, deceived, and killed, and many will abandon their faith, deny Jesus. Jesus warns that only those who endure or remain faithful, will be saved, or enter in the Kingdom of God.

In another parable, Jesus tells his followers in John 10:9, *"I am the door. If anyone enters by Me, he will be saved, and will go in and out and find pasture."* Jesus refers to himself as the *door or gate.* In other words, the true believer will only enter the Kingdom of Heaven through Jesus. What does it mean to enter through Jesus? In John 10:27-28, Jesus said, *"My sheep hear my voice, and I know them, and they follow me: And I give unto them*

[240]

eternal life; and they shall never perish, neither shall any man pluck them out of my hand." The sheep are the believers who obey and follow Jesus. The rewards for obedience are protection from the enemy and eternal life. In Psalm 118, 19-20, King David pleads with God, "*Open to me the gates of righteousness: I will go into them, and I will praise the LORD. This gate of the LORD, into which the righteous shall enter.*" Notice, only the righteous or holy will enter the gates of heaven. In Revelation 22:14, Jesus said, "*Blessed are they that do his commandments, that they may have right to the tree of life and may enter in through the gates into the city.*" Again, only those who follow Jesus' commandments will enter the Kingdom of God and inherit eternal life.

The *road that leads to life* is a difficult path or journey. It involves denying oneself and submitting to Christ, and few people choose the narrow road of obedience. Many Christians have settled for the temporary pleasures and distractions of this world; they have relied on their good works and religiosity for salvation, but Jesus warns his followers in Matthew 7:21 that "*Not everyone who says to Me, Lord, Lord, shall enter the kingdom of heaven, but he who does the will of My Father in heaven. Many will say to Me in that day, 'Lord, Lord have we not prophesied in Your name, cast out demons in Your name, and done many wonders in Your name?' And then I will declare to them, I never knew you; depart from Me, you who practice lawlessness!"* These are Christians who did many good works but did not obey His commandments. They practiced *lawlessness* or transgressed against the law or commandments. Jesus declares harsh words, *"I never knew you"* to mean that this group of people were never really saved. In John 14:15, Jesus describes the true follower, *"If a man love me, he will keep my words: and my Father will love him, and we will come unto him, and make our abode with him."* In other words, Jesus and the Holy Spirit will come and dwell in the heart of the one who obeys Jesus' words or commandments.

The Temple of God

It is so important to understand that God, the Holy Spirit, wants to dwell (live) with mankind. From the beginning, God's plan was to live among His people: In Exodus 29:46, God tells Moses, *"They will know that I am the Lord their God, who brought them out of Egypt, so that I might dwell among them. I am the Lord their God."* In fact, God's promise for the end-time church is that Jesus will return to reign for a thousand years, and *"Behold, the tabernacle of God is with men, and He will dwell with them, and they shall be His people. God Himself will be with them [and be] their God* (Revelation 21:3). It is God's desire (heart) to live and interact with His people. He wants to be a part of our daily lives.

In the OT, the Holy Spirit anointed Kings and prophets to lead or guide His people. In other words, God anointed and assigned His Holy Spirit to some people to fulfill His purpose on earth. The Spirit came upon that person to equip or empower him or her for service to carry out God's plans. King Saul, for example, was anointed by the Prophet Samuel to lead Israel. In 1 Samuel 10: 6, the Prophet Samuel instructs Saul, *"Then the Spirit of the LORD will rush upon you, and you will prophesy with them and be turned into another man."* After God rejected King Saul, the Prophet Samuel took the horn of oil (representing the Holy Spirit), poured the oil over David's head, and *"the Spirit of the LORD came powerfully upon David"* (1 Samuel 16:13). The very next verse records, *"Now the Spirit of the LORD had departed from Saul, and an evil spirit from the LORD tormented him"* (1 Samuel 16:14 NIV). King David was anointed and empowered by the Holy Spirit to defeat the Philistines and rule over Israel.

In the NT, the disciples were filled with the Holy Spirit and given boldness to preach the gospel everywhere. Jesus said to them *"But you shall receive power when the Holy Spirit has come upon you; and you shall be witnesses to Me in Jerusalem, in all Judea and Samaria, and to the end of the earth"* (Acts 1:8). At Pentecost, the Holy Spirit came down as a rushing wind and tongues of fire, and Peter immediately began to preach to the crowd that had gathered outside; many in the crowd were stirred or *"cut to the heart"* by the message. In that day, three thousand souls were saved and baptized (Acts 2:38-44). Hence, the work of the Holy Spirit is to bring conviction of sin and repentance unto salvation: *"For godly sorrow produces repentance leading to salvation, not be regretted; but the sorrow of the world produces death"* (2 Corinthians 7:10). Once saved, we become living temples: *"Know ye not that ye are the temple of God and that the Spirit of God dwelleth in you?* (1 Corinthians 3:16) and *"What? Know ye not that your body is the temple of the Holy Ghost, which is in you, which ye have of God, and ye are not your own? For ye are bought with a price: therefore, glorify God in your body, and in your spirit, which are God's* (1 Corinthians 6:19-20).

The Commandments of Jesus

The LORD made it clear that only those who obey His commandments will be saved. This is the narrow gate: obedience to Jesus' commandments. For example, God made a blood covenant with Israel through circumcision, and issued the Law or Ten Commandments; those who transgressed the Law were severely punished or put to death; in the New Covenant, Jesus shed his blood for our sins; thus, meeting the requirement of the Law (a soul that sins must die). In Matthew 5:17, Jesus said, *"Do not think that I have come to abolish the Law or the Prophets; I have not come to abolish them but to fulfill them."* The word fulfill in Thayer's Greek Lexicon means to *perform, satisfy, carry out and cause God's will (as made known in the law) to be obeyed as it should be, and God's promises (given through the prophets) to receive fulfilment.* As children of God, we should obey and respect God's commandments (laws) and authority. Jesus said, *"If you love me, keep my commandments* (John 14:15). Jesus also said that whoever obeys His commandments will have eternal life and enter the Kingdom of Heaven (Revelation 22:14).

The Greatest Commandment

One day, a lawyer asked Him a question, testing Him, and saying, *"Teacher, which is the great commandment in the law?* Jesus said to him: *"You shall love the Lord your God with all your heart, with all of your soul, and with all of your mind. This is the first and great commandment.* (Matthew 22:36-40). Here, Jesus summarizes the Law. But what does it mean to love God with all your heart, soul, and mind? In this verse, the heart refers to the seat of thoughts, passions, desires, and affections. In Matthew 6:21, Jesus said, *"For where your treasure is, there your heart will be also."* What is treasure? According to Strong's definition, treasure refers to wealth or valuables, so Jesus explains that we spend our time and money on our passions, affections, or desires. Therefore, the message here is that we should give our hearts (treasure) to God: *"You will seek me and find me when you seek me with all your heart"* (Jeremiah 29:13).

According to Strong's definition, the soul refers to our will and emotions. To love God with all our soul, refers to total submission of our mind, will and emotions. How do we submit our mind, will and emotions? We command our soul to submit to God. In other words, we simply ask God (Holy Spirit) to take control: *"Trust in the LORD with all your heart and lean not on your own understanding; in all your ways submit to him, and he will make your paths straight"* (Proverbs 3:5-6).

The Second Greatest Commandment

> *"And the second is like it: You shall love your neighbor as yourself. On these two commandments hang all the Law and the Prophets" (Matthew 22:39-40).*

How do we love our neighbors as ourselves? We ask God to give us a new heart. When God dwells with us, he removes the stony heart and gives us a new heart and spirit: "*I will give you a new heart and put a new spirit in you; I will remove from you your heart of stone and give you a heart of flesh*" (Ezekiel 36:26). This is also a reference to the Holy Spirit. It is only through the power of the Holy Spirit that we can love: "*We love because he first loved us,*" (1 John 4:19) Jesus tells us that the only way to stay in His love, is to keep the commandments: "*As the Father has loved me, so have I loved you. Abide in my love. If you keep my commandments, you will abide in my love, just as I have kept my Father's commandments and abide in his love*" (John 15:9-17). Jesus then commands his disciples to love one another: "*This is my commandment, that you love one another as I have loved you. Greater love has no one than this, that someone lay down his life for his friends.*"

https://www.pewresearch.org/fact-tank/2017/04/05/christians-remain-worlds-largest-religious-group-but-they-are-declining-in-europe/

CHAPTER TWELVE

The Baptism of the Holy Spirit

"He will baptize you with the Holy Spirit and fire." – *Matthew 3"11*

Toward the end of Jesus' earthly ministry, he charged his disciples to expect the *gift* the Father promised. What is the *gift?* It is the power of the Holy Spirit. *"If you then, being evil, know how to give good gifts to your children, how much more will your heavenly Father give the Holy Spirit to those who ask Him?"* (Luke 11:13). In the Book of Acts, we read about the manifestation and *baptism of the Holy Spirit* in the lives of the disciples: The Holy Spirit descended with a violent wind and fire, and they were all filled with the Holy Spirit:

"When the day of Pentecost came, they were all together in one place. Suddenly a sound like the blowing of a violent wind came from heaven and filled the whole house where they were sitting.

> *They saw tongues of fire that separated and came*
>
> *to rest on each of them. All of them were filled*
>
> *with the Holy Spirit and began to speak in other*
>
> *tongues as the Spirit enabled them" (Acts 2:1-4).*

In this chapter, I will address a key question about the Holy Spirit: Who is the Holy Spirit? How does He manifest himself and what is His function or role in our lives?

The Holy Spirit

The Holy Spirit is the third member in the triune nature of God, who comes to reside in Jesus Christ's true followers. He is also referred to as the spirit of truth:

> *"I will ask the Father, and He will give you another*
>
> *Helper, that He may be with you forever' the Spirit*
>
> *of truth, whom the world cannot receive, because*
>
> *it does not behold Him or know Him, but you know*
>
> *Him because He abides with you, and will be in*
>
> *you. I will not leave you as orphans; I will come to*
>
> *you."*

When a person becomes born again by believing and receiving Jesus Christ, his spirit man is reborn and sealed by the Holy Spirit. The Holy Spirit comes to live inside to convict us of sin and guide us in all truth.   In other words, the Kingdom of God is within us: *"Neither shall they say, Lo here! Or lo there! For, behold, the kingdom of God is within you" (Luke 17:21).*

Power of the Holy Spirit

We also see the works of the Holy Spirit or the manifestation of God's power through the lives of the disciples. In Matthew 10:1, Jesus gave his disciples authority to drive out unclean spirits and to heal every disease and sickness. The power of the Holy Spirit represents authority and dominion on Earth over all the power of the enemy: "*I have given you authority to trample on snakes and scorpions and to overcome all the power of the enemy: nothing will harm you*" (Luke 10:19). Jesus' sacrifice restored our *authority or power* over the visible (material) and invisible (spiritual) world.

The power of the Holy Spirit is manifested through the gifts of the Spirit. For example, there are spiritual gifts Jesus gives to the church body such as a word of wisdom, a word of knowledge, increased faith, the gifts of healing, the gift of miracles, prophecy, the discernment of spirits, diverse kinds of tongues and interpretation of tongues as a manifestation of the Spirit (1 Corinthians 12:4-10). God has appointed different

[251]

ministries and diversities of activities to the church or body of believers such as the apostles, prophets teachers, miracles, gifts of healings, helps, administrations, varieties of tongues to establish the Kingdom of God on earth. As believers, we are to earnestly desire the gifts of the Holy Spirit, but Paul points to a more excellent pursuit—the pursuit of love.

> *"Though I speak with the tongues of men and of angels, but have not love, I have become sounding brass or a clanging cymbal. And though I have the gift of prophecy, and understand all mysteries and all knowledge, and though I have all faith, so that I could remove mountains, but have not love, I am nothing. And though I bestow all my goods to feed the poor, and though I give my body to be burned, but have not love, it profits me nothing" (1 Corinthians 13:1-3).*

So how do we pursue love? Paul is talking about becoming mature in Christ. This means *"putting away childish things"* and walking in love. We are to put away the works of the flesh and be led by the Holy Spirit.

Purpose of the Holy Spirit

First, the Holy Spirit convicts us of our sin: *"And when He has come, He will convict the world of sin and of righteousness, and of judgment" (John 16:8)*. True repentance leads to salvation. A sign of the baptism or the work of the Holy Spirit is a deep conviction of sin, followed by repentance and a desire to please God. Second, the Holy Spirit is our advocate or counselor who leads us into a deeper knowledge of the truth, intercedes on our behalf and provides divine strength during trials. Jesus describes the role of the Holy Spirit as the Helper and Teacher: *"But the Comforter, which is the Holy Ghost, whom the Father will send in my name, he shall teach you all things, and bring all things to your remembrance, whatsoever I have said unto you."* (John 14:26). Thirdly, the function of the Holy Spirit is to guide us into all *truth*: *"But when he, the Spirit of truth, comes, he will guide you into all the truth. He will not speak on his own; he will speak only what he hears, and he will tell you what is yet to come"* (John 16:13); thus, the Holy Spirit leads us into a deeper relationship and walk with Jesus to redeem and set us free: *"Then, you will know the truth (Jesus), and the truth (Jesus) will set you free"* (John 8:32). *To know* means to have intimate knowledge or be known.

To have a relationship with Jesus, means freedom from the power of sin. Thus, Jesus set us free from the power of sin, and the Holy Spirit works to sanctify and transform us into the image of God: *"And the Lord—who is the Spirit—makes us more and more like him as we are changed into his glorious image"* (2 Corinthians 3:18). The Holy Spirit is God abiding in us to carry out His will on earth and to make us one with the Father. In fact, Jesus prayer for His disciples and believers was that they would also be one (spirit, soul and body) with the Father just as He was one with the Father: *"I pray that they will all be one, just as you and I are one—as you are in me, Father, and I am in you. And may they be in us so that the world will believe you sent me"* *(John 17:21).*

Sealed or Marked

At conversion, we are sealed or marked by the Holy Spirit: *"And who has also put his seal on us and given us his Spirit in our hearts as a guarantee."* but we do not receive *the full measure* or sevenfold characteristics of God. We are sealed (marked) or baptized by the Holy Spirit for the restoration and redemption of the soul. *"And you also were included in Christ when you heard the message of truth, the gospel of your salvation. When you believed, you were marked in him with a seal, the promised Holy Spirit" (Ephesians 1:13).* Unless you reject and renounce Christ as your savior, or sin willfully, the Holy Spirit remains in you forever: *"And I will ask the Father, and he will give you another advocate to help you and be with you forever"* (John 14:16). As we continue to grow in Christ, we receive more of the Spirit or power.

This power is a supernatural manifestation of his presence. God comes to live inside of you and manifests His glory through you. The old testament describes the tabernacle of Moses and how the Shekinah glory rested in the Holy of Holies as a pillar of cloud by day and a fire by night to guide them. The Glory of God represents the presence of God manifested. The Holy Spirit comes to indwell in tabernacles of clay (human bodies), and we are to surrender ourselves to his guidance. *"Don't you know that you yourselves are God's temple and that God's Spirit lives in you? (1 Corinthians 3:16).* In fact, this is the purpose of our creation: that we become living tabernacles (temples) of God: *"Everyone who is called by my name, whom I created for my glory, whom I formed and made"* (Isaiah 43:7 *NIV).* We were formed in His image to become one with Him for His glory (Shekinah glory). How is this accomplished? For us to become one with Christ and the Father, we must die to self and surrender our will. This is the only way. Paul said it best, *"I have been crucified with Christ, and I no longer live, but Christ lives in me" (Galatians 2:20).*

Dying to self is a hard concept to comprehend in our Western culture. It does not mean dying physically but dying to our desires, lusts, plans and yes—our dreams. This culture feeds us the lie that we can shape our destiny, satisfy our desires, or fulfill our dreams, but the truth is, that this is not what God had in mind for our lives. In other words, this is not what we were created for in this life. The Bible says, *"For my thoughts are not your thoughts, neither are your ways my ways," declares the Lord (Isaiah 55:8).* Our way of life demands that we satisfy all our desires. We have grown so accustomed to having our needs met that we rarely think about how selfish and deprived we really are. We are so consumed by self that we have selfies to prove it on social media platforms, and yet, there is a vast number of people reaping the fruits of selfishness or self-indulgence and suffering from depression, suicidal thoughts, addictions. Our flesh seeks out entertainment, pleasure, and satisfaction, but the fruits of this lifestyle, lead to death, dissatisfaction, emptiness, and despair. If you look at the message of the Gospel, we were not meant to indulge our flesh 24/7 but to deny it. How do we deny our flesh?

If you study the life of Paul, you see someone who not only struggled with sin, but with his flesh (pride). Paul uses very graphic language to describe this battle, *"I batter my body and bring it into servitude lest having preached to others, I myself might be disqualified" (1 Corinthians 9:27 Berean Literal Bible).* Paul doesn't beat his body but brings it under subjection to the spirit. In other words, he practices self-control and restraint. Some Bible scholars believe that Paul *beat* his body into submission or practiced self-flagellation; however, this is not necessary, since Jesus Christ bore our sins on the cross and shed his precious blood to set us free from the penalty of sin. We do not need to bruise our bodies to rid ourselves of sin, we simply repent and turn to Jesus for the remission of our sins. Many in the Catholic church believe that self-denial involves vows of poverty or chastity, but this goes contrary to the Word of God as well. We must deny (suppress, resist) our evil nature, selfish will or inclinations, thoughts, and tongue. This has more to do with the condition of our hearts than any outward changes we make. Sometimes, we need to rid ourselves of material possessions or renounce *mammon* (the root of evil) to truly walk in holiness. If we submit to the will of the Holy Spirit, we will conquer our flesh and sin, and live like Jesus. This is the work of the Holy Spirit—to sanctify and transform our nature—to become like Jesus.

Meditations and Prayer to Receive the Baptism of the Holy Spirit

[Read the Scriptures aloud several times]

To You, O LORD, I lift my soul. O my God, I trust You; Let me not be ashamed; Let not my enemies triumph over me. Indeed, let no one who waits on You be ashamed; Let those be ashamed who deal treacherously without cause. Show me Your ways, O LORD; Teach me Your paths. Lead me in Your truth and teach me, For You are the God of my salvation; On You I wait all day. Remember, O LORD, Your tender mercies, and Your loving kindnesses, For they are from of old. Do not remember the sins of my youth, nor my transgressions; According to Your mercy remember me, For Your goodness' sake, O LORD. Good and upright is the LORD; Therefore, He teaches sinners in the way. The humble He guides in justice, And the humble He teaches His way. All the paths of the LORD are mercy and truth, To such as keep His covenant and His testimonies. For Your name's sake, O LORD, Pardon my iniquity, for it is great. Who is the man that fears the LORD? Him shall He teach in the way He chooses. He himself shall dwell in prosperity, And his descendants shall inherit the earth. The secret of the LORD is with those who fear Him, And He will show them His covenant. My eyes are ever toward the LORD, For He shall pluck my feet out of the net. Turn

Yourself to me, and have mercy on me, For I am desolate and afflicted. The troubles of my heart have enlarged; Bring me out of my distresses! Look on my affliction and my pain and forgive all my sins. Consider my enemies, for they are many; And they hate me with cruel hatred. Keep my soul and deliver me; Let me not be ashamed, for I put my trust in You" (Psalm 25:1-20).

Prayer to invite the Baptism of the Holy Spirit

LORD, you are my salvation and my refuge. I will trust in you. You restore my soul and guide me in the paths of righteousness for your name's sake (Psalm 23:3). Search me, O God, and know my heart, try me, and know my thoughts. And see if there be any wicked way in me and lead me in the way everlasting (Psalm 139:23-24) I renounce sin and submit to your will. Create in me a clean heart, O God, and renew a right spirit within me (Psalm 51:10). Cast me not away from thy presence; and take not thy holy spirit from me (Psalm 51:11). For your word says that if I confess with my mouth that Jesus is LORD and believe in my heart that God raised Him from the dead, I will be saved (Romans 10:9) and he that believeth on me, out of his belly shall flow rivers of living waters (John 7:38). I ask for the baptism of the Holy Spirit, for your word says that if we being evil know how to give good gifts unto our children; how much more shall our heavenly father give the Holy Spirit to them that ask him?

[259]

(Luke 11:13). Your word promises that Jesus will baptize me with the Holy Spirit and fire (Matthew 3:11). Breathe on me, Jesus, and I will receive your Holy Spirit (John 20:22).

Made in the USA
Coppell, TX
28 June 2023

18577299R00144